Faculty of Arts
University of Helsinki

GENERATING CREATIVE LANGUAGE - THEORIES, PRACTICE AND EVALUATION

DEPARTMENT OF DIGITAL HUMANITIES

THE DOCTORAL PROGRAMME FOR LANGUAGE STUDIES

Mika Hämäläinen

DOCTORAL DISSERTATION

To be presented for public discussion with the permission of the Faculty of Arts
of the University of Helsinki, on the 28th of October, 2020 at 13:00 o'clock. The
defence is open for the audience through remote access.

Helsinki 2020

Advisors: Jack Rueter and Jörg Tiedemann
Pre-examiners: Tony Veale and Hugo Gonçalo Oliveira
Opponent: Tony Veale
Faculty representatives: Tuomo Hiippala and Krister Lindén
Custos: Jörg Tiedemann

https://mikakalevi.com
https://rootroo.com

The Faculty of Arts uses the Urkund system (plagiarism recognition) to examine all doctoral dissertations.

ISBN 979-869-44-5462-9 (nid.)
ISBN 978-951-51-6706-4 (nid.)
ISBN 978-951-51-6707-1 (PDF)

Helsinki 2020

ABSTRACT

This thesis presents approaches to computationally creative natural language generation focusing on theoretical foundations, practical solutions and evaluation. I defend that a theoretical definition is crucial for computational creativity and that the practical solution must closely follow the theoretical definition. Finally, evaluation must be based on the underlying theory and what was actually modelled in the practical solution.

A theoretical void in the existing theoretical work on computational creativity is identified. The existing theories do not explicitly take into account the communicative nature of natural language. Therefore, a new theoretical framework is elaborated that identifies how computational creativity can take place in a setting that has a clear communicative goal. This introduces a communicative-creative trade off that sets limits to creativity in such a communicative context. My framework divides creativity in three categories: message creativity, contextual creativity and communicative creativity. Any computationally creative NLG approach not taking communicativity into account is called mere surface generation.

I propose a novel master-apprentice approach for creative language generation. The approach consists of a genetic algorithm, the fitness functions of which correspond to different parameters defined as important for the creative task in question from a theoretical perspective. The output of the genetic algorithm together with possible human authored data are used to train the apprentice, which is a sequence-to-sequence neural network model. The role of the apprentice in the system is to approximate creative autonomy.

Evaluation is approached from three different perspectives in this work: ad-hoc and abstract, theory-based and abstract, and theory-based and concrete. The first perspective is the most common one in the current literature and its shortcomings are demonstrated and discussed. This starts a gradual shift towards more meaningful evaluation by first using proper theories to define the task being modelled and finally reducing the room for subjective interpretation by suggesting the use of concrete evaluation questions.

In Memoriam

Respecting the memory of my mother Irma Hämäläinen, who passed away when I was 14 years old, my dog Lunni, who passed away at the age of 12, and my sister Mari Latto, who passed away last year.

CONTENTS

LIST OF ORIGINAL PUBLICATIONS

This thesis is based on the following publications:

I   Hämäläinen, M., & Alnajjar, K. (2019). Generating Modern Poetry Automatically in Finnish. In *2019 Conference on Empirical Methods in Natural Language Processing and 9th International Joint Conference on Natural Language Processing: Proceedings of the Conference* (pp. 6001–6006). Stroudsburg: The Association for Computational Linguistics.

II   Hämäläinen, M., & Alnajjar, K. (2019). Modelling the Socialization of Creative Agents in a Master-Apprentice Setting: The Case of Movie Title Puns. In *Proceedings of the 10th International Conference on Computational Creativity* (pp. 266-273).

III   Hämäläinen, M., & Alnajjar, K. (2019). Let's FACE it: Finnish Poetry Generation with Aesthetics and Framing. In *12th International Conference on Natural Language Generation: Proceedings of the Conference* (pp. 290-300). Stroudsburg, PA: The Association for Computational Linguistics.

IV   Hämäläinen, M., & Honkela, T. (2019). Co-Operation as an Asymmetric Form of Human-Computer Creativity. Case: Peace Machine. In *Proceedings of the First Workshop on NLP for Conversational AI* (pp. 42–50). Stroudsburg: The Association for Computational Linguistics.

V   Hämäläinen, M., Partanen, N., Alnajjar, K., Rueter J. & Poibeau T. (2020). Automatic Dialect Adaptation in Finnish and its Effect on Perceived Creativity. In *Proceedings of the 11th International Conference on Computational Creativity*. (pp. 204-211)

VI   Hämäläinen, M., & Rueter, J. (2018). Development of an Open Source Natural Language Generation Tool for Finnish. In *Proceedings of the Fourth International Workshop on Computational Linguistics of Uralic Languages* (pp. 51-58). Stroudsburg: The Association for Computational Linguistics.

The publications are referred to in the text by their roman numerals.

ABBREVIATIONS

BRNN	bi-directional recurrent neural network
CC	computational creativity
E2E	end-to-end
FST	finite state transducer
GA	genetic algorithm
GAN	generative adversarial network
IPA	international phonetic alphabet
LSTM	long short-term memory
NLG	natural language generation
NLP	natural language processing
NMT	neural machine translation
RNN	recurrent neural network
seq2seq	sequence-to-sequence

1. INTRODUCTION

Creativity has puzzled philosophers from the times immemorial. Unsurprisingly, it has provoked a whole deal of theoretical work aiming to capture what the phenomenon is really about dating all the way back to Plato (see Asmis, 1992). In fact, Gaut (2012) divides philosophical takes on creativity into two categories: irrationalism and rationalism. Plato belongs to the former category, which assimilates creativity with madness or intuition. However, Plato would consider art requiring craftsmanship rational. Rationalism highlights creativity as an act requiring reasoning such as planning a plot so that it elicits certain emotions in the reader.

Moving away from the previous dichotomy, one of the most cited theories on human creativity in the computational contexts is the four Ps by Rhodes (1961). According to this view, creativity consists of person, process, product and press. Person refers to the psychological traits and capabilities such as intelligence, attitudes and values of a creative individual. Process highlights the importance of how something is created rather than focusing only on what is created, namely the product. Press describes the wider sociocultural context, or environment, where creativity takes place.

Most importantly, creativity is something that we have considered fundamentally human (cf. Hennesey & Amabile, 2010) for a long time in the history of mankind. Yet, what is considered creative, is inherently socially constructed. For instance, Shao et al. (2019) report that usefulness is considered more important for creativity in the East, while in the West novelty is considered an equally or more important attribute of creativity. There seems to be a tendency for people to think that creativity should only occur in the biological. Pease & Colton (2011) have called this ideology carbon fascism based on the critique on machine creativity expressed by Bedworth & Norwood (1999).

This thesis presents my research on creative natural language generation (NLG). This research is conducted within the paradigm of computational creativity. Colton and Wiggins (2012) characterize the discipline as, "the philosophy, science and engineering of computational systems which, by taking on particular responsibilities, exhibit behaviours that unbiased observers would deem to be creative", a definition which has later become one of the most fundamental ones in the field.

The establishment of computational creativity as a field of research took place over a decade ago, and this year the major conference dedicated solely on the field,

ICCC (International Conference on Computational Creativity) reaches its 11th annual iteration. Furthermore, the first call for papers of the Journal of Computational Creativity was announced as recently as last year. Despite this relatively long time frame, I have identified two major drawbacks that have not been solved to a satisfying degree. Firstly, there is a plethora of practical work on generative systems and a great deal of theoretical papers describing computational creativity. There is, however, a gap between the two; practice is hardly ever motivated by theories. Secondly, evaluation has always been the Achilles' heel of the research conducted on the field (see Lamb et al. 2018).

In this thesis, I will further elaborate on the two problems and my take on advancing the state of affairs with respect to both of them. I will show results from following the current practices (paper I) and present two different creative systems based on two different theoretical points of view (papers II and III). I will show the shortcomings of the current evaluation methods (paper V). Furthermore, I will present a theoretical framework of my own to fill a theoretical void in the field (paper IV). In order to solve NLG challenges for Finnish on a practical level, I have authored an open-source library (paper VI).

The major technical contribution of my dissertation is the introduction of the master-apprentice approach, which joins the interpretability of a traditional machine learning approach, namely that of a genetic algorithm (GA), with the flexibility and adaptability of a neural network. What makes the GA interpretable is that it uses several different fitness functions each of which measures a different desired attribute. Both of these approaches serve a purpose for the overall system. In this thesis, I will argue for interpretability of the aesthetics the system follows in order for it to satisfy the requirements set for computational creativity. However, such a system is oftentimes rather static and cannot be autonomous in its creativity, hence I combine it with neural networks that can learn to adjust their standards more freely based on the training data.

Whereas my work methodologically follows the similar empirical machine learning as a great majority of current NLP research does, I would like to draw more attention into the question of evaluation throughout my thesis. In a field that relies heavily on automated methods, human evaluation is often conducted in an ad-hoc fashion without questioning what such an evaluation can or is supposed to reveal about a given computational system. Therefore, I propose more reasoned ways of approaching the problem of evaluation, especially in papers II and III.

2. THEORIES OF COMPUTATIONAL CREATIVITY

In the field of computational creativity, a myriad of different theories has emerged that try to identify what computational creativity exactly is or should be. The theories focus on creativity from a computational perspective, rather than the perspective of what creativity means when exhibited by people.

I myself do not agree with the argument that computational creativity should not be the same as human creativity. However, it is true that with the current state of computational models, computers cannot be creative in the exact same fashion as real people, but this is, by no means, a maxim of computational creativity. What I do agree with, is that we should not approach computational creativity from the same theoretical perspective as we approach human creativity. Mostly due to the fact that a lot is still unknown about human cognition and how creativity actually emerges in us, despite extensive theoretical work, whereas how we are modelling creativity in machines is very much known to whoever seeks to build a creative system.

Computational creativity research has tried to deviate itself from any research focusing on generation, such as regular NLG research. A pejorative term *mere generation* has been used in the field pointing out that systems that are not creative, are just *merely generating*. However, the term itself could be better defined and it seems to mean different things for different authors, and the most authoritative and cited source for the term is a blog post by Veale[1] that is unavailable at the time of writing in the original url.

What I understand by *mere generation* and how I would define it is that the system does not operate on any definition of creativity. As I have already pointed out in the introduction, creativity is an inherently socially constructed concept. It means different things to different people at different times. For anyone to argue that their system is creative, they must also state what they mean by creativity itself. For as long as no definition is provided, anything goes for as long as it produces output convincing enough to fool people into seeing more than what the intention of the system ever was (see. 5. On Evaluation of Computationally Creative Systems for more)

---

[1] https://web.archive.org/web/20170402185912/http://prosecco-network.eu/blog/scoffing-mere-generation

If a definition for creativity is provided, the problem becomes easier to model, and it becomes easier to critically assess the degree to which a system is creative (see Alnajjar & Hämäläinen, 2018). This thinking is at the core of my thesis and it is reflected by papers II and III. Mainly, the key idea is based on the SPECS approach (Jordanous, 2012), which states that creativity must be first defined on an abstract level, and then on a concrete level. Finally, the evaluation of the system should be in line with the initial definitions.

I do agree with the ideas presented in the SPECS approach, but I find the definition for creativity proposed in the paper troublesome (see 2.5. SPECS for more). Furthermore, I think that an additional requirement for the SPECS ideology is needed; that is an alignment between the definition, implementation and evaluation. One can have an apt definition and a suitable evaluation for the definition, but if the implementation does not even try to reflect what has been defined, the evaluation results are hardly representative of the creativity of the system (see 5. On Evaluation of Computationally Creative Systems for more elaboration on this thought).

The remainder of this section is dedicated to presenting some of the existing, influential theories on computational creativity. The most crucial sections for my thesis are sections 2.3.-2.5. as they serve as the theoretical foundation of my work in papers II and III, although some of the ideas of Section 2.1. are present in paper II and the overall ideology presented in Section 2.2. is remotely touched in paper I. Section 2.7. Asymmetric Creativity and Conveying a Message is dedicated to describing my theoretical work on filling a theoretical void in the existing computational creativity theories as described more profoundly in paper IV.

Creative autonomy, as defined by Jennings (2010), requires three components for a system to be considered autonomous in its creativity. The system should be able to evaluate its own creations without external judgment, change its own standards without being explicitly told how to do so, and none of the first two requirements may rely on pure randomness. The work presented in papers II and III approximates this notion with the master-apprentice framework.

2.1. BODEN ON CREATIVITY

There is no doubt that Boden (2004) is one of the most celebrated takes on what it means to be creative within the computational creativity paradigm. Two ideas of hers are raised time after time in computational creativity research. The first is a simple dichotomy that divides creativity into two categories according to the novelty value: P- and H-creativity.

P-creativity, or psychological creativity also known as personal creativity, is any kind of creative innovation that is only novel to the creator itself. Essentially this means that if a person figures out how to solve a puzzle, such as a Rubik's cube, they are exhibiting P-creative behavior as many people before them have solved the same puzzle in the past and many people will continue to do so in the future.

If the novelty value reaches to a more global context, we are dealing with H-creativity, which is human or historical creativity. This means creativity that is a game changer in the way of thinking and is unlikely to occur often by different people. An example of this is the use of fire which revolutionized the history of mankind.

In paper II, I am, however, assimilating H-creativity with a more down to earth and easier to achieve creative behavior. Mainly due to the fact that the paper deals with humor generation and a joke, no matter how good, can hardly be contrasted to an achievement of the nature of the fire. Therefore the H-creative is seen more as something non-obvious i.e. something people would not come up with easily by themselves or have not heard before.

The other set of important notions Boden introduced have to do with how the creative process unfolds. These are *exploratory, transformational* and *combinational creativity*. The latter of which is often not seen as important as the first two, and is for instance, omitted in the later formalization of Boden's three-fold definition (see 2.2. Formalization of Boden's Theories). Combinational creativity is related to coming up with something new by combining familiar concepts. A good example would be an analogy, which can be used to explain something unfamiliar with familiar terms.

Exploratory creativity is related to the idea that there is a conceptual space that consists of creative artifacts. Exploratory creativity is similar to conducting a search in a search space (=conceptual space). The search space can consist of complete or partial solutions. In this sense, the poems one can create are all found within the search space where creative thought occurs. Nothing outside of the space can be created.

As exploratory creativity is clearly limited by the bounds of the search space, there are only so many things one can create. A change in the rules that define the search space introduces a paradigm shift. This is known as transformational creativity as it transforms/changes the space where creativity occurs and thus enables us to come up with completely new solutions that were not available in the original search space, such as completely different kinds of poems.

I have intentionally used the word *search space* here instead of the original wording *conceptual space* to draw a closer link between these notions and genetic algorithms (GA), a model that we have employed in papers I, II and III. I will provide a more detailed link between the GA and these notions in the following section.

2.2. Formalization of Boden's Theories

In order to better situate Boden's concepts of exploratory and transformational creativity in the field of computational creativity, Wiggins (2006) has presented his formalization and extension on the two notions. He begins his argumentation by introducing the concept of a universe. The universe contains everything possible, from the desired creative artefacts to artefacts of a completely different nature. A conceptual space is then defined within the universe for conducting creative search. Such a space is selected by an interpretation function by applying rules that define the space. For example, a context-free grammar might be such an interpretation function that sets the limits to what can be generated according to its rules. In other words. it can never generate sentences that are not covered by its rules.

In addition to rules defining the search space, Wiggins identifies another set of rules that are used to traverse it. A context free grammar can be run to generate all the possible sentences, or the search space can be traversed in a more informed fashion by following heuristics of some sort.

When the system conducts search, or traverses the conceptual space, it needs an evaluation function to assess the quality of the concepts it finds. This is important so that the system can know when it has found a creative artefact of a value, as the search space is bound to contain many bad solutions. These are the requirements for exploratory creativity.

For transformational creativity, the system needs to be able to change the way in which it conducts the search. This can be done in two ways, either by changing the rules that define the search space or by changing the rules that are used to traverse it. While Wiggins states the possibility of changing the evaluation functions as well, he does not describe that possibility extensively.

In terms of the GA, there is quite an overlap in these theoretical notions. Without going too deep on the technicalities that are to follow in Section 3.3. The Master-Apprentice Approach, GA conducts search by mutating and crossing individuals over with each other. At the end of each generation, the individuals are evaluated, and the fittest ones are left to survive for the next generation. The possible

14

search space is defined by the initial individuals and how the mutation and crossover are implemented. In our master-apprentice framework, the transformational creativity is left for the apprentice, as the search space can change depending on the training data used. Different variations of the training data are discussed in papers II and III.

2.3. THE CREATIVE TRIPOD

Colton (2008) presents a computational creativity framework called the creative tripod. The tripod has three legs: *skill*, *imagination* and *appreciation*. Creativity cannot occur without all three legs being present simultaneously. This theory is important for my thesis as it is the foundation of the work presented in paper II.

Skill means the capability of performing the creative action, producing an artefact. A painter will have multiple techniques in his arsenal, or a sculptor will know how to shape a statue out of marbel. Skill itself does not yet entail creativity; if a highly skilled painter copies an existing painting with the highest attention to detail, he still does not achieve creativity according to the tripod.

Imagination refers to the fact that creativity is not supposed to be repetitive. A degree of novelty is needed in the created artefacts. A skillful painter painting the same painting over and over again is hardly creative. I would like to point out the similarity of the concept of imagination with Boden's P- and H-creativity, both of which essentially relate to the novelty of the created artefact. This assimilation is also presented in paper II.

Appreciation is the last leg of the tripod. It simply refers to the capability of assessing one's own creations. A generative system can easily produce a lot of artefacts (high imagination) based on a skill learned from data. However, such a system is still not creative unless it can appreciate its own output. Furthermore, in paper II, I argue that appreciation should be nuanced reflecting the individual attributes that constitute humor rather than a single probabilistic value. I would also like to point out the similarity with the evaluation function described in Section 2.2. Formalization of Boden's Theories.

The creative tripod identifies that computational creativity is a joint effort between the programmer, the computer and the consumer, each of which can bring their effort to the overall creativity of the system. My view on this, which I also hold in paper II, is that the system must exhibit all of the legs of the tripod. Nonetheless, the degree to which they come from the programmer is another question. In paper II, the master inarguably exhibits all the different legs of the creative tripod to the extent they were defined to produce humorous headlines. This is due to the fact that the fitness functions and how they operate has been defined by us, the programmers. The situation gets more difficult for the apprentice, which is not defined by a programmer per se, but the data it learns from. In such a case, the presence of a programmer is considerably smaller, but the degree to which appreciation is exhibited by the system becomes much less clear. For the future, I would propose an extension to the creative tripod framework taking the training data into account as well as one of the contributing factors to the creativity of the system. This theoretical extension will allow for a better inspection of the effect of the training data.

It is inevitable that the consumer is an important party in the creative act of the system. Computational creativity is typically interested in producing pleasing, artistic artefacts, which are meant to be consumed by people. However, any system that completely outsources any of the legs of the creative tripod to the consumer, cannot be creative in my view. This point will become evident in Section 5. On Evaluation of Computationally Creative Systems.

2.4. FACE

FACE (Colton et al, 2011) identifies four components that should be present in a computationally creative system: *framing*, *aesthetics*, *concepts* and *expression*. All of these can be characterized on the ground level and process level i.e. what they are and how they came to be. This theory is particularly important for paper III, as it serves as its theoretical basis. I will describe these components in an inverse order from the most concrete to the most abstract.

On the ground level, expressions are the output, the artefacts created by the system. This simply means artefacts such as poetry or humor. On the process level, expressions are the output for a given input to a concept.

Concepts are easiest to understand as programs, for on the ground level, the term refers to the creative program that produces expressions. On the process level, the question becomes how the program was made. This is fundamentally related to my earlier discussion in Section 2.3. The Creative Tripod, that is, how much of the concept is due to the efforts of the programmer and how much due to the data used to train the system.

Aesthetics is close to the evaluation function of Wiggins (2006) and appreciation of the creative tripod (Colton, 2008). Again, the system should be able to assess the aesthetic value of its own creations on the ground level. On the process level, a similar question raises as in the case of concepts. What is the degree to which the aesthetic measures are defined by the programmer and by the data.

The last notion of the theory, framing, is what sets it clearly apart from other theories on computational creativity. Framing is a co-text that is to be presented together with the creative artefact, such as a description of the author's life or a similar side note typically seen in art museums next to a painting. Framing can be used for multiple purposes such as for persuading people into believing in creativity of the system by providing more historical or cultural context. The use of framing for deception is also discussed in Cook et al. (2019) among other uses. In our work presented in paper III, I reject the use of framing for such a purpose. The way framing is used there is to expose the internal aesthetic measures for the purpose of human evaluation. Therefore, the use of framing is only to provide the information the system had during the creative process, not to come up with an insincere background story or interpretation.

It is important to note that one thing that is usually associated with creativity, namely novelty, is completely missing from this framework. I state this to further highlight how differently creativity can be understood and defined, even by contemporary theories.

2.5. SPECS

The main ideology of the SPECS approach (Jordanous, 2012) was already discussed in the introductory text of this main section, namely that the approach requires creativity to be defined on an abstract level, then on a concrete level reflecting the particular creative task in question, and finally the evaluation of the system should be based on the definitions. However, the approach comes with its own, preferred, definition for creativity. Here I will describe it and explain why it is not adequate for my main argument of an alignment between theory, implementation and evaluation. SPECS lists altogether 14 key points for creativity.

A creative system should have a deliberate effect on the creative process and it should be able to cope with uncertainty and incomplete answers. There should be domain competence and general intellect present in the system. I find the term general intellect especially challenging as a starting point for a definition of a creative system. If defining creativity is a challenging task, using intellect as one of the terms to define it, opens up another equally difficult to define concept. In fact, there is a lot of debate in the field of artificial intelligence about what it really means to be artificially intelligent (see McCharty, 2007).

According to SPECS, the system should be able to generate results or reach a goal in a novel way, and do so in an independent way. There should be personal or emotional involvement or intention or desire to perform a task. This requirement, again, is one that is very difficult to model computationally. In fact, there is an entire field of science dedicated to modelling emotions computationally with a multitude of different theoretical starting points (see Marsella et al., 2010).

Furthermore, the SPECS states that there should be progression and development in the process and creativity should take place in a social environment. Subconscious processing and thinking as well as evaluation are also mentioned as important factors of creativity. However, again, in order to argue for subconsciousness or thinking in a creative system, one first has to deal with the problem of computational consciousness. The problem is that currently, there is no agreement on the nature of human consciousness either, whether it simply emerges from a complex system or is a feature of the biological brain fully explainable by the firing of the neurons (see Kim, 2018).

Finally, the approach states that there should be value and variety in the output. The main reason I do not think that this 14 point definition for creativity can be used as a starting point for any computationally creative system is that it includes terminology that is fully human (such as emotions, consciousness, intelligence) and the computational modelling of which is a challenge equally difficult to creativity, if not more so. Especially if one seeks to have the problem definition, implementation and evaluation in line, implementing and evaluating these notions becomes difficult if not impossible.

2.6. Co-Creativity

In this section, I will briefly describe some of the theories on co-creativity, that is a scenario where a human is engaging with a creative system. This section serves mainly as a background for the following section, where I present my own theoretical extension to this line of theoretical work. Lubart (2005) identifies four different scenarios for co-creativity where a computer acts as a: nanny, pen-pal, coach or colleague.

In a nanny situation, the computer sets deadlines and guides the user in a creative task. This does not require too much creativity from the computer, but rather functionalities related to keeping the user's work effective and organized. In a pen-pal scenario, the computer is more of a platform that enables the exchange of creative ideas. Again, such a system does not need to exhibit any creative behavior of its own. A computer acting as a coach can help the user in engaging in creative thinking by displaying information in novel ways. In this situation, the system does not need to exhibit creativity on its own, but it certainly needs to know about creativity in order to promote and propagate more creative thinking. Finally, if the computer acts as a colleague, it is in a real partnership with the human user, as a creative equal.

Davis (2013) introduces the concept of human-computer co-creativity that aims to bring HCI and computational creativity closer to each other. This notion adheres to the ideology of having a computer as a colleague in the creative process. In this view, the computer should be able to adapt and react to the input provided by the user in creative and novel ways. The interaction sequence can be unpredictable and does not need to follow a specific script, which makes the task of coping with such input more demanding for the machine.

Mixed-initiative co-creativity, a notion elaborated by Yannakakis et al. (2014) is also a manifestation of a computer as a colleague. The important aspect is that the two parties, the human and the computer, can actively participate in the creative behavior, but not necessarily to the same extent. They demonstrate this theory in the context of a game designing system.

2.7. ASYMMETRIC CREATIVITY AND CONVEYING A MESSAGE

In this section, I present the overall theoretical contribution of paper IV. The existing theoretical work on co-creativity highlights that there is always human creativity present, and computational creativity may or may not be present, on the one hand. On the other hand, computational creativity theories usually highlight aesthetics or value of the output ignoring the most fundamental function of human language; communication.

We humans hardly ever sit on a chair in a corner of a room and generate aesthetically pleasing utterances with no understanding or intention behind the message we want to convey with our words. An exception to this might, of course, be a patient suffering from Wernicke's aphasia, but in the broad sense, we usually verbalize something we want to communicate. In my work, I have called any effort of generating language without a message, a meaning to convey, mere surface generation in the spirit of mere generation. I am not claiming that my practical work (papers I, II or III) or any other work on computational creativity I am aware of is trying to be anything beyond mere surface generation. Nevertheless, it is important to subject this notion to theoretical inspection.

Based on the discussions I had when presenting this paper, I feel the need to clarify what I mean by conveying a message. For instance, Loller-Andersen & Gambäck (2018) present a system that can produce poetry about an image given to the system. The argument against mine was that the system does have a message, that is the content of the image. Now, going back to my previous example of a person sitting in a corner and uttering pleasing sentences, even if these sentences were about an image and somewhat related to it semantically, it still does not entail any message in particular; anything even remotely related fills the purpose. For instance if we say, "it is raining outside", we probably want to communicate the meaning of a particular kind of weather occuring outdoors rather than communicating something about a picture of an umbrella. It is not uncommon to have an input for a creative system that is used to generate output related to it (c.f. Veale & Alnajjar 2016; Gervás, 2018; van Stegeren & Theune, 2019). For my theoretical work, however, communicating about something is not the same as communicating something.

As it is difficult to grasp what it would even mean for a computer to have a message that it needs to communicate, especially in very artistic text generation, such as poetry, stories or movie scripts, without resorting to an unnecessary degree of anthropomorphism, I have decided to take goal-oriented dialog under my theoretical inspection. In such a system, even though there is no internal motivation for a computer to communicate its inner thoughts (whatever those might be), there is typically some information content that needs to be communicated, such as the timetable for a train or the price of plane tickets. Although there is a lot of practical work done on dialog generation/adaptation relating to the field of computational creativity (c.f. Shen et al. 2017; Wei et al. 2018; Hämäläinen & Alnajjar, 2019; Chikai et al., 2019), the approaches usually fail to demonstrate that the intended message (if any) is conveyed as intended and that there is creativity in the process.

In the paper, I commence describing my theoretical framework by presenting existing related theories in an interdisciplinary fashion. Moreover, I identify the main limiting factors, that is the maxims of the co-operative principle (Grice, 1975), as the core of the framework. In order to ensure that the goal oriented dialog system still excels at conveying its message effectively, it should follow the co-operative maxims: manner, quality, quantity and relevance. I incorporate other theoretical notions and their interdependencies to the model reaching a framework that sets the limits the system has to fulfill regardless of its supposed creativity.

I identify a communicative-creative trade off. If a system optimizes communication of the desired message as purely and fully as it is required by the context, only very little room is left for creativity. In contrast, if the system goes to the other extreme of creativity, it will probably try to communicate the message very creatively, for example, as a riddle, which jeopardizes the understandability of the message in the recipient. Knowing the limits to how creative and how communicative the system needs to be is contextually dependent and requires understanding of the user, a user-model in other words. Thus a balance between creativity and predictability must be maintained.

In order to better know how creativity can manifest itself in a conversation governed by strict linguistic, cognitive and social rules, I identify three types of creativity that can occur in a conversational setting: message creativity, contextual creativity and communicative creativity.

Message creativity can occur in the level of altering the denotation of the message. For instance, the expressions *a glass is half empty* or *half full* communicate essentially about the same phenomenon, yet their denotations are very different. A system can purposefully alter what it sets to communicate for as long as the same idea gets through. It is possible for the system to seek to alter the connotation of the message as well. If the context allows, the system can opt for a formal or for a more casual wording of the message delivering different connotation, for instance, about social distance or emotional affect. Finally, the system can purposefully exploit the speech acts (see Searle, 1969), for example in order to communicate an expressive message with a directive surface form.

The notion of contextual creativity gives a lot of room for creative exploration of the context. It partly relies on a user model that can enable computational approaches to intersubjectivity, namely if the system knows the user well enough, it can predict whether certain devices of figurative language, such as metaphors or sarcasm, will be understood as intended by the user. As we typically take a role in conversation (see Goffman, 1959), a system can actively try to shift its role for something that enables more creativity if the context permits that. Finally, the system can take the time perspective of the conversation into account and either conduct creative planning of the future directions of the conversation or bring up past events of the conversation in a new light.

Communicative creativity can occur by selecting a new social script for the conversation that allows for more creativity. It is also important to adjust the level of elegance that the system aims for in the conversation. Elegance is understood as the most minimalistic way possible for conveying a message as fully as possible. In conversation, aiming for minimalism might rule out a lot of the creative potential that the system could otherwise unlock. Finally, the system can also deviate from the co-operative maxims in an informed way. The system can communicate more than what is necessary, for instance, if the communicative output still contributes to the conversation.

The theory is asymmetric in the sense that it does not expect any creativity to be present in the human user, but only in the computational system. The paper includes an adaptation of the theoretical model to the Peace Machine thinking as elaborated by Honkela (2017). The main focus of the Peace Machine is to challenge AI for social good, and especially in contributing to the process of peace by enabling creative thought, meaning negotiation and enhanced intersubjectivity. The goals of the system are, however, beyond the scope of my dissertation.

3. PRACTICAL APPLICATIONS

This section is dedicated to describing the existing practical work on the two main tasks of computational creativity presented in papers I-III. In addition, I present the practical solutions taken in my papers in this section. I do not yet take any stance on the theoretical aspect of my work for how the theories and practice intertwine is presented in section *4. From Theories to Practice*.

3.1. RELATED WORK ON HUMOR GENERATION

Humor generation, and pun generation in particular, has received quite some attention in recent years. Automated humor detection has also provoked some research interest (Yang et al., 2015; Bertero et al., 2016; Chen & Soo, 2018) as more and more annotated data have become available such as the recent Humicroedit dataset from last year (Hossain et al., 2019). However, as humor detection typically operates on a particular dataset learning the particular humor in that specific dataset, it is quite a distant task from generation, especially since generation of the creative kind is supposed to produce something novel and unexpected as well. Although detection/appreciation is a key part of creative generation, I will not describe approaches dedicated purely to detection in this section as their starting point is typically different from that of generation. In this section, I will focus more on the recent humor generation systems, for an overview across a longer timespan, see paper II.

Humor generation has been approached from two different disciplines during the past few years. On the one hand there are the researchers within the computational creativity (CC) paradigm who try to model creativity or at least novelty in their approaches, on the other hand, there are people in the field of NLP who have proposed systems from a merely generative standpoint. I will start by describing some of the recent approaches arising from the field of NLP before moving to the discourse taking place in CC.

Aggarwal & Mamidi (2017) propose a system generating *Dur se dekha* jokes in Hindi. These jokes follow a predefined structure similar to knock-knock jokes in English. Their method is based on hand written templates and a manually collected lexicon. They use three constraints to pick a suitable punchline from the lexicon: semantic category, grammatical gender and form constraint expressed by rhyming or Levenshtein distance. They evaluated their system on a 5-point Likert scale by consulting 15 people, and their system achieved nearly human-level in naturalness (3.16 vs 3.33), but scored only mildly on the humor aspect (2.4).

A deep learning take on homographic pun generation was proposed by Yu et al. (2018). They use a conditional LSTM based language model to generate a punny sentence that has both of the desired senses for an input word present at the same time. They use the English Wikipedia with word sense disambiguation labels predicted by an existing tool. They evaluate their system by consulting only 5 people on Amazon Mechanical Turk. Their system achieved results that are considerably lower than human authored puns but higher than their baseline system on the abstract scale of fluency, accuracy and readability.

Luo et al. (2019) present a method for generating polysemous puns by using a GAN approach. Their model consists of a generator that can produce a punny sentence containing the desired word in two senses, and a discriminator that can predict the real and punny senses of the output of the generator. The generator is trained on Wikipedia data that is automatically tagged with word-sense disambiguation tags. They evaluate their approach using only three annotators. The results of their model were clearly preferred over puns generated by an existing model (57 times vs 24 times), however, human authored puns were preferred almost all the time to the puns generated by their system (79 times vs 8 times).

He et al. (2019) present a system for generating homophonic puns based on a local-global surprise principle. They argue that a pun word should be surprising in a local context and congruent in the global context. In other words, the punny word should seem like a misfit based on the semantics of words that are in its immediate neighbourhood, but still make sense in the level of the whole text. They use a language model to assess the surprise introduced by a punny substitute word. Their system takes in an existing sentence, replaces a word with a punny one and modifies the sentence to support the meaning of the punny word even further. They report that as few as 31% of the puns generated by their system were rated as puns by people on Amazon Mechanical Turk.

The recent work conducted within the computational creativity domain has focused on a variety of different types of humor. Whereas the NLP research is mainly interested in purely ML driven E2E solutions, the CC field finds more use in templates and human intuition when designing the system.

Humor generation in the context of memes in Portuguese has been studied by Gonçalo Oliveira et al. (2016). The system turns headlines into memes by picking a suitable meme image and adapting the headline to a meme like format. For mapping a headline to a meme image, a rule based classifier is used. Headlines are adapted to meme text by either finding a similar proverb based on semantics or rhyming. Predefined templates are then used to render the final meme text. They evaluated the system on a 5-point Likert scale based on coherence, suitability, surprise and humor by altogether 52 people, on the average the score for coherence was 3.81, while for the other 3 metrics the average was closer to 3 (2.98, 3.06 and 3.10 respectively).

A system producing sarcasm that can potentially exhibit humor is presented by Veale (2018). The presented system tries to produce a failure in expectation contradicting a salient property of a concept for sarcastic effect; this is done by consulting existing semantic databases that link concepts to their properties, adjectives to nouns in other words. The system exploits carefully designed templates and rules in sarcasm generation. The paper argues that systems designed for analysis cannot simply be reversed to generate, as an analyzer can yield results due to over-fitting without truly generalizing to understand the phenomenon. The paper presents a study of perceived positivity of the focal word by human judges, but it does not present any evaluation of the full sarcastic sentences.

Winters et al. (2019) proposes a system that generates humor based on schemas that tell the system how the joke should be generated by defining the generator function, template, metrics, aggregator and keywords. The metrics used for humor generation are obviousness of a word (its corpus frequency), conflict in the punchline (n-gram probability), word compatibility (n-gram probability as well) and inappropriateness (corpus frequency). They evaluate the system on a star rating with 203 people 11.41% of the jokes generated by their system got 4 or more stars as opposed to 21.08% for human authored jokes.

The work proposed in paper II does not only differ from the existing work based on the technical approach and theoretical foundation embraced, but also the problem setting is very different. While there is existing work on pun generation, our approach does not rely on polysemy or homonymy (complete or partial), but rather takes a more flexible approach in sound similarity. In addition, the task is more specific as our system does not reach a satisfactory output by producing any sentence containing a desired pun, but rather it has to produce a recognizable movie title delivering a pun.

3.2. RELATED WORK ON POEM GENERATION

Poem generation has a long tradition in computational creativity research (see Gonçalo Oliveira, 2017). Recently, it has also started to gather more interest in the NLP community, most notably by Chinese NLP researchers. In this section, I will first describe some of the recent work conducted on the field of NLP before describing more computational creativity oriented research. It is to be noted that NLP research on poetry does not limit only to generation, but also covers poem analysis (see Kao & Jurafsky 2012; Caccavale & Søgaard, 2019; Rahgozar & Inkpen, 2019).

Zhang et al. (2017) propose a memory augmented neural network model, which, according to their claims, produces more innovative poems than previous neural approaches to Chinese poetry generation. They train an RNN based model with attention to generate poems from input topic words on corpora of Chinese poetry. The output of the system is evaluated by 34 experts based on compliance (rhymes and tones), fluency, aesthetic innovation and scenario consistency on a 5-point Likert scale. From the different models they experimented with, none was clearly the best on all the parameters, but the highest individual average scores were 4.1, 3.01, 3.07 and 3.17 respectively. They do not report the results for theme consistency per model although they stated it as an evaluation criterion.

Lau et al. (2018) model sonnet meter and rhyme as a joint neural model. They train their model on automatically tagged data. The model consists of three LSTM models, a language model, an iambic meter model and a rhyme model, all of which are trained together in a multi-task learning setting. In their human evaluation, they removed the workers who did not perform well enough in control questions. The evaluation task was to distinguish a human written poem from a computer written one. Their best model was indistinguishable from human written poetry 46.8% of the time. However, their expert evaluation suggested that their model was only good at rhyming and meter, while falling short on readability and emotion.

Reinforcement learning has been proposed by Yi et al. (2018). They use the criteria previously used in human evaluation fluency, coherence, meaningfulness and overall quality as reward functions for the algorithm. They train two reinforcement learning models that also learn from each other. In their human evaluation, they recruit 12 experts so that each poem will get 3 different evaluations. They report relatively high scores (between 3.6 and 4.06 on the average) for their best model.

Yang et al. (2019) model poem generation as an unsupervised machine translation problem. Their system takes text written in vernacular Chinese as input and produces a poem in classical Chinese as output. They use an existing unsupervised machine translation approach that consists of an encoder-decoder architecture. They have 30 people evaluate their system based on fluency, semantic coherence, semantic preservability (how much of the meaning of the vernacular Chinese text is preserved in the translation) and poeticness. They use a 5-point Likert scale, resulting in average scores higher than 2 but lower than 2.7 for their best dataset. The approach merely paraphrases poetry from one domain to another and it does not generate novel outputs at each run.

In more of the computational creativity side of research, Manurung et al. (2012) propose a genetic algorithm approach to generating poetry. In their approach, they define that a system must satisfy three criteria for poems; grammaticality, meaningfulness and poeticness. Grammaticality is set as an absolute constraint in the GA. They use a derivation tree grammar formalism as a basis for the generated poetry, the trees are mutated by adding or removing a random subtree during the genetic process. Subtrees may also be swapped by the mutation or crossover. Poeticness is evaluated by comparing the meter of the individual poems to a target meter and meaningfulness is evaluated by semantic similarity to the target semantics. They only conduct evaluation by automated metrics rather than consulting human evaluators.

Gonçalo Oliveira & Alves (2016) present an approach for generating poetry from text by first extracting a conceptual map from the input and then adapting the semantic network used in generation to the extracted concepts. The generator itself consists of multiple modules that have been designed to do different tasks such as line generation or organizing lines in the poem. They elaborate a specific grammar formalism to convert the conceptual map to a form suitable for poem generation. The system can rank its generation candidates based on rhyme and meter. The authors do not present any automatic nor human evaluation of their system.

An n-gram based method has been elaborated by Gervás (2017) to produce poetry that caters for thematic consistency and enjambment in a template free fashion. The paper highlights the problem that existing work usually focuses on a particular aspect of poetry and solves that from an engineering point of view, while this focus is never explicitly stated and the work itself gives the impression as though the much larger problem of good poetry generation was solved to a greater degree. Therefore, this particular paper makes a narrow focus admitting that any features beyond those explicitly solved (thematic consistency and enjambment) are solely due to serendipity and not to the system's internal capabilities. I completely agree with this argumentation and papers II and III hold a similar stance towards CC. The approach by Gervás (2017) uses a corpus to determine word relatedness and vocabulary for rhymes. A generative n-gram model is used to generate sentences that are picked for the poem if they satisfy the requirements of word relatedness and rhyming. The results are evaluated with human judgement counting the number of thematically consistent words over the total number of words and open line transitions over all line transitions. This evaluation strategy relies on one person's opinion.

Twitter tweets can be combined into poems as suggested by the approach taken by Lamb et al. (2017). Their system groups tweets in their twitter corpus into categories based on their mutual rhyming. As they are focusing on sonnets, they remove all tweets that do not fill the syllabic criteria of a sonnet from the corpus as well as tweets that do not rhyme with any other tweet. Their system can rate tweets based on an emotion lexicon, trigram frequency and an imagery lexicon. They evaluated their system on a 5-point Likert scale using the following questions: *How much do you like this poem? How creative is this poem? How well does this poem express the emotion of [emotion]? How meaningfully does this poem summarize its topic? How new and different is this poem? How new and different is this poem? How cohesive is the narrative of this poem?*. The average values for each question were between 2 and 3.5. Interestingly, they did not perceive a significant difference between expert judges and non-expert judges.

A great deal of the previous work on poem generation has been mostly interested in superficial features, such as rhyme, meter and surface-level semantics, or just training a model to mimic poetry for the sake of it being trained on poems in hopes of the model learning the essence of poetry automatically. While our system in paper I does not extend far from the superficial, the poem generator in paper III has a more nuanced set of aesthetics that capture a wide range of characteristics typical to poems. Furthermore, neither of the systems is trained on poetry per se albeit they do use existing poems as templates. Especially important is the shift in the research focus in paper III from the output to the internal appreciation of the system.

3.3. THE MASTER-APPRENTICE APPROACH

The practical foundation of the systems presented in paper II and III is on the master-apprentice framework. This means that there are two interacting systems in place, a GA-based master and a seq2seq RNN-based apprentice. The work presented in paper I only consists of a single agent, a GA. The first version of the master-apprentice was developed by us in an earlier paper not included in this dissertation (Alnajjar & Hämäläinen, 2018). One advantage of the approach is that while the master can only generate a certain kind of output as defined by the evolutionary process, the apprentice can learn to extend from it by human authored data. In this way, the apprentice will not only mimic what humans have created, because part of the training comes from the master, neither will it only resonate the outcomes from our evolutionary algorithm as human authored data is also present.

3.3.1. MASTER AS A GENETIC ALGORITHM

In the papers, we model the master by using the same genetic algorithm implementation. The major differences between the papers are in the fitness functions and parameters for the genetic process. In addition, the poem generators in paper I and III differ in the initial population; the approach presented in paper I uses different poems in the population, whereas in III the whole population is initialized with the same poem. In this section, I will describe how the genetic algorithm operates in more detail.

We use a GA implementation provided in the DEAP library (Fortin et al., 2012). The algorithm is a standard $\mu + \lambda$ implementation. It operates on a population μ producing an offspring λ. During the process, mutations and crossovers will occur and the individuals in each generation are ranked based on the fitness functions using NSGA-II non-dominant sorting (Deb et al., 2002). NSGA-II is designed to rank individuals based on multiple parameters, as each individual is scored based on multiple metrics in the fitness function, ranking them becomes non-trivial.

In the very beginning, the algorithm needs an initial population. This population is based on existing artefacts. For movie title puns, it means that the initial population will be initialized with the movie title that is supposed to be converted into a punny form, for poetry generation, the population is initialized with existing poetry.

The population undergoes an evolutionary process for the desired number of generations. The evolutionary process has a great deal in common with the idea of modelling creativity as a search (c.f. Wiggins, 2006). The GA produces new individuals from existing ones by mutating them, the mutation has been implemented in a slightly different fashion in each paper, but in practice, the GA picks one word in an individual and replaces it with another one. Two individuals can also be selected for crossover, which in our papers means selecting one point in

29

the two individuals and swapping what follows after that point. The new individuals are added to the offspring produced by the current population.

At the end of each generation, a selection takes place. All individuals both in the current population and in the offspring are scored based on the fitness functions defined in each paper. The top fittest individuals are picked to survive to the next generation. It is important to note that the selection selects individuals from the current generation and the offspring. This ensures that if a good individual has been produced at some point during the evolutionary process, that individual is kept from generation to generation until better ones are produced. Otherwise, the quality of the individuals could degrade drastically over one generation if none of the new ones were on par with the previous ones.

For the Finnish language, the mutation does not merely replace words with others without any reference to grammatical knowledge as this would easily result in incomprehensible sentences. The system operates on lemmas that it will inflect to the morphology of the original context by using Omorfi (Pirinen, 2015) on UralicNLP (Hämäläinen, 2019). While this mostly solves the morphosyntactic requirements known as agreement, it does nothing to solve case government. For the case government, we use a practical NLG tool presented in paper VI.

For a better illustration of how the GA picks the best individuals for the next generation, I will describe some of the fitness functions used in the different papers. Please refer to papers I-III for full description of all the fitness functions used. The fitness functions range from the simple rule-based to more complex neural models. The simplest one that is common for both puns and poetry is the existence of rhyme in its various forms (full rhyme, consonance, assonance and alliteration). In poetry, the fitness functions measure the number of rhyming within the poem whereas for pun generation it is calculated between the original word and the potentially punny replacement word. For Finnish, we can determine rhyming easily with rules by looking into the characters of a word as the Finnish writing system is very phonetic.

For English, many existing approaches use CMU dict or ryhmes from Wiktionary to overcome the fact that the written form of words in English is not particularly phonetic. However, our initial master-apprentice approach (Alnajjar & Hämäläinen, 2018) needed something more robust as our system was dealing with words related to Saudi Arabia, some of which were direct loans from Arabic. This called for a more robust approach that can cover even atypical loan words. This is why our English rhyming mechanism uses a popular speech synthesizer eSpeakNG[2]

---

[2] https://github.com/espeak-ng/espeak-ng/

to convert English words into IPA. This makes it possible to determine rhyming with simple rules even with the difficulty resulting from the English writing system.

To capture sentiment in poetry, we use an already existing recent state of the art approach (Feng & Wan, 2019) as one of the fitness functions. The approach made it possible to train a sentiment analyzer for Finnish without annotated data in Finnish. Their method relies on training the model with English data and using bilingual word embeddings to predict sentiment for Finnish as well. The fitness function measures the variance of the sentiments within an individual poem, while preferring the values for variance learned from a poem corpus.

3.3.2. APPRENTICE AS A SEQ2SEQ MODEL

In our initial work on the master-apprentice approach (Alnajjar & Hämäläinen, 2018), there was only one master and one apprentice. The goal was to model computational creativity in the master so that it could produce creative movie title puns on its own. The apprentice was trained on the data produced by the master and human written movie title puns of the same domain, that is Saudi-Arabia related puns. The key idea behind having an apprentice is to permit the system to achieve the requirements for creative autonomy (see Jennings, 2010), that is, it can change its standards from what has been explicitly programmed into the master, while not fully relying on mere replication of human authored artefacts.

As the master operates on modifying an existing input (a movie title or a poem) and producing an output based on it, the task can equally be modelled as a sequence-to-sequence problem. The apprentice in papers II and III is a recurrent neural network (RNN) trained on a popular tool for training neural machine translation (NMT) models, known as OpenNMT (Klein et al, 2018).

The master-apprentice setting is extended in paper II to simulate different learning scenarios how the master teaches its apprentice. The scenarios were inspired by research on developmental psychology, more concretely we modelled the parenting styles identified by Baumrind (1991). The parenting styles can be divided into four categories, authoritarian, authoritative, rejecting-neglecting and permissive parenting, each of which was modelled as a different way the training of the apprentice took place.

Paper III extends this by introducing two different masters into the equation. This work does not rely on any psychological findings in human behavior but is more of a modest extension to how the master and apprentice have been utilised in the past. Furthermore, the difference this paper has regarding the previous work is that the apprentice is not trained on human authored data as such data is not present for the task of Finnish poem generation by using existing poems as a starting point. In this work, creative autonomy is not approximated with the help of human authored data, but ultimately, by following two different masters.

4. FROM THEORIES TO PRACTICE

A definition of the problem one is set to solve is important when modelling anything computationally. Especially when the object of interest is something as elusive as creativity. For creativity can mean multiple different things to different people and without defining it before tackling it by computational means is like walking in a dark maze; disoriented, without any way of telling whether any of the steps taken have brought you anywhere nearer to the main goal.

In some more established fields of NLP, the problem definition is by no means needed to be explicitly stated, as they have established automated evaluation metrics. Therefore, the problem statement becomes more of "take any means necessary to get high scores on gold annotated data". This has led to a field that focuses more on the numerical truth of automated evaluation metrics than on advocating for a deep understanding of the real-life phenomenon being modelled. Nevertheless, automated evaluation metrics, however poor they might be (see for example Reiter, 2018; Talman & Chatzikyriakidis, 2019), make it possible to measure progress. It can now be said whether the steps taken in the dark maze have led closer to the exit or not.

Computational creativity research, it should be noted, typically does not explicitly define the problem that is being solved. Even if a definition is given, it is usually only for the sake of the technical implementation, and it is hardly given any reasoning as to why the particular definition was chosen and especially why it should model anything creative apart from purely generative. As a remark, Pollak et al. (2016) have found that the conceptualization of computational creativity, while exhibiting some stability, also changes over time, which highlights a part of the problem of researching creativity without defining it first.

I do like the ideology presented in the SPECS approach (Jordanous, 2012), and according to it, creativity must first be defined on an abstract level and then on a concrete level. I would also like to defend that any computational implementation of a creative system must try to address explicitly the requirements set in this definition; this is something overlooked by SPECS. Otherwise, the fact of having a definition loses its meaning. In the current era, it would be perfectly possible to come up with an elaborate definition of what poetry should be and just train a GAN model on raw poem data. If there is no alignment between the definition and the implementation, it becomes impossible to say to what degree the problem was

33

solved at all. It might very well be the case that the GAN just recycles solutions to the problem from human poets without creating anything of its own.

In the following sections, I will elaborate the theoretical foundations presented in paper II and III for humor and poem generation. Having an established definition of the problem to be solved makes it possible to track progress and evaluate the systems in a more meaningful way. Without any definition for creativity in poem generation, for example, any system capable of spitting out strings that resemble poetry would be sufficient.

4.1. HUMOR GENERATION

The abstract level definition for creativity in general was chosen to be that of the creative tripod, and more particularly focusing on the three legs of the tripod: skill, appreciation and imagination. In order to bring these notions to the context of humor generation, or pun generation, to be precise, it is important to look into what is known about puns and humor in a non-computational setting.

Many theories highlight that incongruity plays a crucial role and its resolution leads to a humorous effect (Oring, 2003; Attardo & Raskin, 1991). In practice, it means that two different scripts have to be possible at the same time, and they need to be in opposition (Raskin, 1985). However, a more concrete take on humor is that it requires surprise and coherence (Brownell et al., 1983), and we follow this definition in our approach. This theory does not completely deviate from the rest as surprise is close to the notion of incongruity, and coherence is what makes the resolution of surprise/incongruity possible.

The task itself of generating food related puns is not made up by us, but is based on a movement that took place on Instagram where people came up with food related puns out of existing movie titles, similarly to our system, such as *Harry Potter and the Deathly Marshmallows* instead of *Harry Potter and the Deathly Hallows*. These real-world puns authored by real people give us on the one hand, a narrowed down task to model, and on the other an additional source of training data for the apprentice.

We define that in order for the system to exhibit skill, it should be able to make a punny version out of an existing movie title in such a fashion that the original movie title still stays recognizable. These requirements for creativity are modelled in different parts of the system. The initial population of the master is initialized only with one original movie title to ensure the puns will be made for that specific title. One of the fitness functions measures the number of altered words in the movie title,

34

as the more words are altered, the more difficult it becomes to recognize the original movie title. Another fitness function is set to measure rhyming to ensure that the word replacements meet the minimum requirement of a pun, that is a sound similarity.

Now, for a pun to be funny, something more is needed. The appreciation the system has should be able to assess humor as it was defined based on existing theories. For this reason, fitness functions for evaluation of surprise and cohesion are implemented as they are needed for a joke to be funny. The fitness function evaluating sound similarity is part of the appreciation as well, as it not only tells that there is sound similarity, but also the degree to which it occurs.

The last requirement for creativity is imagination, which we define to be at least P-creativity in the output, but preferably H-creativity as well. This is taken care of by the genetic process that can find new punny titles novel to itself by mutation and crossover.

It is to be noted that only the implementation of the master is meant to reflect all the necessities for computational creativity in this particular context. The role of the apprentices is just a mere approximation of creative autonomy of the overall system when both the master and the apprentice are seen as a single whole. This is mostly since the apprentice is capable of learning both from the computationally creative master and human peers.

In relying on a theoretical foundation, we have made certain that there is a clear definition of what we are trying to solve, instead of just claiming to solve humor generation as a whole. Furthermore, it is possible to see a link between the theory and practice as what was being modelled corresponds to the individual parts of the definition. If a better way of solving any of the subcomponents of creative movie title pun generation emerged, it could be integrated to the current master presumably improving the quality of the output.

4.2. POEM GENERATION

In the context of paper III, creativity was first defined through the FACE model. In other words, the key components of creativity are now framing, aesthetics, concept and expression. Although we use these notions to define computationally creative poem generation, we do so only in the context of our poem generator. We do not seek to model poetry as a whole, as coming up with a definition capable of stretching over the whole genre of poetry is an endeavour too difficult even for those engaging in the practice of literary studies.

The expressions the system needs to produce are Finnish poems. Their creation is heavily guided by the aesthetics of the master. For the apprentice, they are produced by the sequence-to-sequence mappings it has learned from the input-output pairs of the master. All in all, for generating a new expression, an existing human authored poem is given as an input, and the expression output by the system is a new poem based on modification to the input.

On the level of concepts, there are masters and apprentices. Masters are programmed and designed by us, but they can adjust their appreciation based on a corpus. Apprentices are trained on the data of their masters. This means that there is a higher degree of flexibility in what these concepts are to become than what there is in the masters. Even more so, if they were to be exposed to human written parallel data.

The most crucial part for creativity lies in the aesthetics. These aesthetics are modelled as fitness functions in the master. The apprentice learns to mimic to a degree the qualities measured by these aesthetics in its output. The aesthetics followed are divided into four categories: sonic, semantic, imagerial, and metaphorical.

For the sonic aesthetics, the system must be able to appreciate the existence of rhyme, assonance, consonance or alliteration. In addition, the system should aim for maintaining the meter of the input poem. The meter is calculated by the number of syllables and the foot measured by the distribution of short and long syllables in each verse. This way, the system is not fixed to a certain meter for all poetry, but can flexibly use the meter that was in the input poem.

Semantics in poetry are different from those in everyday language and themes can vary within a poem drastically. This means that not all the words in a poem need to seem like they would fit into the same semantic fields. In fact, dividing words of a poem into their different semantic fields can reveal tensions and hidden interpretations of the poem (c.f. Lotman, 1974). Therefore, the system divides words into clusters by their semantic similarity by using affinity propagation (Frey & Dueck, 2007). The distances between the clusters are contrasted to the distances the master has learned from a corpus to know how distant two clusters must be and how distant they can be.

Imagery is an important aspect of poetry (see Kantokorpi et al., 1990), and in practice it refers to the mental images the act of reading a poem can evoke in its reader. In the philosophy of mind, these mental images are known as qualia (see Chalmers, 1995), and they are indeed considered a hard problem of mentality, far beyond the reach of a mere machine. However, the system should be able to evaluate them with its aesthetics. For this reason, the master implements a fitness function for sentiment analysis in order to get a better grasp of the potential sentiment evoked in the reader. Also, as Kao & Jurafsky (2012) point out echoing the words of Burroway (2007), concrete words can be used to provoke imagery. For this reason, the master also measures the concreteness of the words of a poem to assess its imagery.

The final aspect of metaphors in poetry is assessed by finding metaphorical relations between the semantic clusters of a poem. As poems might have vocabulary that does not form a semantically meaningful whole, they are likely to make sense pragmatically, i.e. through interpretation of figurative language such as the metaphor. Metaphors can be understood as consisting of a tenor and a vehicle (Richards, 1936). The metaphoricity of having the centroid of one cluster as a tenor and the centroid of another one as the vehicle is assessed by automatic measures adapted from Alnajjar (2019).

Framing is used in our approach to make the aesthetics used by the master for its poetry more transparent. As it is easy to retrieve the individual values from the different fitness functions for the generated poetry, it is possible to provide a framing by filling a template with slots for the framing information to be provided. This framing is then used when conducting human evaluation, as discussed in the following sections.

5. On Evaluation of Computationally Creative Systems

As we have seen in the related work section, there are many ways of conducting evaluation of systems aiming for creative language generation. Some papers only present automated evaluation, while some conduct a human evaluation. Whatever the evaluation metric, it is usually picked in an ad-hoc manner (see Lamb et al., 2018).

The SPECS approach does state that evaluation should come from the definition of creativity, an idea I could not agree more with. Needless to say, I cannot emphasize enough how important it is that the implementation of the system also try to explicitly model what has been defined. Otherwise one would not be evaluating the effectiveness of the proposed computational solution, but rather whether people are ready to perceive something in the output that the system was not aware of itself. Thus, any merit that the output of the system might have, does not come from the system itself but is due to serendipity, to a mere chance or the characteristics of the corpus used in training.

In fact, Veale (2016) points out that people are ready to interpret a deeper meaning in computer generated text, providing that it has a suitable linguistic form. Such is the case for any system that does not try to model any of the evaluated metrics in particular. Quite many papers, as we saw in the related work section, evaluate poem generation based on metrics such as poeticity or meaningfulness, while the actual implementation focuses merely on enforcing rhyme and meter in a model trained on existing poems. This is cumbersome especially since poems are meant to be interpreted. A seemingly irrational combination of words might gain a deeper meaning when read by humans.

In the next sections, I present the evaluation and my findings from paper I. The evaluation in this paper follows exactly an ad-hoc approach that is more or less the typical way of going about evaluation in CC and creative NLG. In paper V, I show the bigger problems arising from this type of evaluation. I shall also describe the evaluation from paper II that aimed for evaluation based on a model that implements the requirements defined for movie title pun generation. And finally, I will describe the results of paper III, where the aim was also to reduce the possibility of interpretation and people reading more into the output, when evaluating the system.

I am not taking a stance on the question of using expert evaluators versus amateur evaluators. While some findings suggest that there is no difference (Lamb et al., 2017), while others suggest that experts are more consistent (Toral et al., 2018). However, I am afraid this question might be very specific to the task that is being solved and to the solution proposed. Furthermore, experts might introduce another source of bias especially if they have a strong opinion on how a particular kind of art should be, rather than what it could be.

5.1. Ad-Hoc and Abstract

In this section, I will describe the evaluation presented in paper I, and more importantly I will discuss the findings presented in paper V on the same evaluation metric. This section focuses on evaluation with abstract ad-hoc questions.

What I mean by ad-hoc evaluation questions is that the evaluation seems to come from nothing. Usually there is no reasoning behind the evaluation questions or they are taken as such from existing research. Typically they do not try to address the different aspects that are being modelled or are considered important for the problem definition. Such an evaluation can be found to a great extent in contemporary papers dealing with creative NLG, and paper I is no exception.

In this way, it is possible to gather evaluation results that look convincing but do not really tell anything about the system. The evaluation questions used in paper I were, *How typical is the text as a poem? How understandable is it? How good is the language? Does the text evoke mental images? Does the text evoke emotions? How much do you like the text?*, evaluated on a 5-point Likert scale and one binary question *Is the text a poem?*. These questions are very typical ones and they have been used in previous research as well. The problem arises that not unlike in many existing papers out there, the fitness functions of the system only measured different kinds of rhyming, poetic foot and rudimentary semantics. In other words, the system neither attempted, nor was it capable of optimizing for typicality, mental images, emotions or general likability. Out of the evaluation questions, it only aimed for comprehensibility as semantics had been considered during the creative process and grammaticality as the methods presented in paper VI were in place.

Everything else is mainly about the evaluator's ability to read more into the poem than what the system ever intended. This is indeed a problem, especially in the era of neural networks, when it is now easier than ever to train a model to produce good sounding text. The only thing that does matter to evaluation questions of this nature is whether people are ready to read more into the output of the system, to project a deeper meaning to the poem.

I would like to highlight that the initial idea of SPECS is not enough, meaning that evaluation should follow from a definition, but the implementation must also conform to the initial definition. It would not be impossible for me to come up with a definition for creativity for paper I based on the evaluation questions to make the definition and evaluation be in line. But it would still not change the fact that the implementation does not even try to solve a majority of the attributes that are evaluated. Unfortunately this evaluation practice is omnipresent in the field and it makes it next to impossible to compare the different systems proposed over the years.

Abstractness of the evaluation questions is another thing that I have learned to be a matter to avoid. One of the times I was conducting poem evaluation on these very questions, one of the evaluators struggled on the first question, he looked at me with agony on his face and said: "How can you ask something as difficult as this? Is the text a poem? And yet, you are giving me a text without its context, for it is the context that makes a poem a poem!" This moment was revealing, the more abstract the questions, the more room for interpretation there is. Even the question whether something is a poem or not is open to interpretation, to a high degree of subjectivity. And all this would have gone unnoticed had I conducted the evaluation online on FigureEight or Amazon Mechanical Turk. Removing the outliers, as suggested by some, can hardly solve this problem. For example, the person who struggled with the first question answered no differently to the questions than his peers. It is to be noted that people can take very different interpretative strategies in answering the abstract evaluation questions, but these cannot necessarily be seen in the data collected.

I have evaluated my first poem generator (Hämäläinen, 2018) that used rules, knowledge bases and a statistical language model to generate poetry with the same evaluation questions. In the same paper, I also evaluated a method that took full sentences out of a corpus and put them together to form a poem. Both of these methods were able to get better results on most of the metrics in human evaluation than what an existing system had received when it had been evaluated. This perhaps, highlights the problem even further, that even combining poems out of existing sentences with no creative intent, can indeed yield state-of-the-art results.

In paper V, I generated poems with my first poem generator (Hämäläinen, 2018) and converted them into 3 different Finnish dialects automatically. The evaluation was conducted with the same abstract questions, but this time, my intention was not to showcase a new system with claimed computationally creative capabilities, but to see how something as superficial as a dialect can affect the evaluation results. This time, the poems that were not adapted to any dialect got worse results than in my initial evaluation presented in the original paper. This points towards the fact that there is not much stability in using abstract questions over time. One important factor might be that in 2018, none of the evaluators even thought that computers could be used to generate poems, and they felt surprised that they had read poetry with no human author, whereas in 2020, many of the evaluators asked after the study whether the poems were computer generated.

Our findings on dialects suggest that even though dialectically adapted poems scored lower on all the metrics than the original non-dialectal poem generated by the system, there was an observable tendency. The further away the dialect was from the written standard, the lower it scored. This can perhaps point towards a familiarity bias meaning that people are more likely to prefer things familiar to them than those they are unfamiliar with. Based on these evaluation results, we can say that dialect that is usually an uncontrolled variable can affect the results, though negatively. However, dialect can also have a positive effect.

Paper V presents another evaluation, where we asked people to associate words with either the original standard written Finnish poem or its dialectal counterpart. Words *creative* and *original* were considerably more frequently and *poem-like* slightly more frequently associated with the dialectically adapted poem, whereas *fluent* was considerably more frequently associated with the standard written Finnish poem and *emotive* and *artificial* slightly more frequently. This means that if this kind of an association type evaluation was followed, the uncontrolled variable of dialect can make poems to be perceived as more creative and original.

5.2. THEORY-BASED AND ABSTRACT

In paper II, I present my work on moving away from ad-hoc evaluation questions into something more reasoned by the actual approach taken. This involves theoretical definition, a computationally creative system that implements the definition and evaluation questions that are directly derived from the definition. As we will see in this section, this is but a step towards a more meaningful evaluation, but the abstract nature of the evaluation questions continues to pose challenges yet to be tackled.

As described in section *4.1. Humor generation*, the master was tailored to work on the creative tripod framework consisting of skill, imagination and appreciation.

41

For skill, we used the following evaluation statements: *The title has a pun in it, The title is related to food* and *The original title is recognizable*. For appreciation the statements were: *The title is humorous, The pun is surprising* and *The pun makes sense in the context of the original movie*. And finally, the statements for imagination were *The pun in the title is obvious* and *The pun in the title sounds familiar*. The evaluation was conducted on a 5-point Likert scale, higher values indicating more agreement with the statement.

The evaluation statements are measuring the individual aspects that we defined important for the task and implemented in the master. For instance, the statements for appreciation ask about humor and its subcomponents separately, as it was the subcomponents, surprise and coherence, that were explicitly modelled in the system. In fact, in our previous approach (Alnajjar & Hämäläinen, 2018) we found this evaluation sufficient. However, the aspect of having multiple apprentices in paper II quickly revealed the shortcomings of the evaluation.

We ran the same evaluation on a crowdsourcing platform for movie title puns generated by the master and four apprentices in different learning scenarios: authoritarian, authoritative, rejecting-neglecting and permissive. The different learning scenarios can be shortly described so that in the authoritarian scenario, the apprentice only got training data from the master, in the authoritative one, the training data came from the master and from peer data filtered by the fitness functions. In the rejecting-neglecting scenario, the apprentice only learned from peer data and in the permissive one, the apprentice learned from all the data.

Our initial impression when looking at the results by ourselves was that permissive and rejecting-neglecting produced the worst results. This was also supported by our automated evaluation metric that was based on the fitness functions. When looking at the results from the human evaluation, however, this conclusion was no longer as straight forward. In fact, the permissive apprentice got the best scores on recognizability of the original title, making sense in the context of the original movie title, not being obvious and not sounding familiar. None of these metrics result in a high level of humor or punniness, however. Neglecting scored the highest on food relatedness, humor and surprise.

The authoritarian apprentice scored the highest only on punniness and surprise. However, it consistently scores high on all the metrics, as does the neglecting apprentice. As none of the apprentices nor the master is the single best one on all the metrics, it becomes difficult to suggest any model over another. Especially since the authoritative apprentice got the clearly highest score on punniness, which was the ultimate goal of the approach, but scored lower than the neglecting apprentice on the other metrics important for creativity and humor.

The evaluation questions are still abstract and leave room for interpretation. When taking a closer look at the evaluation results for individual annotators, I could see many cases where, for instance, titles that did not have a pun in them in my opinion were rated as punny and vice versa for titles that did have a clear pun. Thus subjectivity and possibility for interpretation are still present with these evaluation questions. Having test questions is not a solution either as they might introduce bias in the selection of human judges. If the judgments of only those who answer "correctly" to test questions are considered, rather than improving the quality of the evaluation, it might ensure that only judges like-minded with us are selected. This would indeed yield the desired results, but do so without any scientific validity.

It is also important to note that the rejecting-neglecting apprentice was only trained with puns authored by humans. Yet it scored high on our evaluation metrics that were supposed to measure computational creativity, not a mere copying behavior. On one hand, this supports my claim that training a model to generate based on data will deliver good results, but it does not reach creativity (at least not by the definition we followed in the paper), on the other hand it highlights a problem in the evaluation metrics and underlines how important it is that the computational model is also explicitly aware of the necessary metrics. All in all, even though this evaluation is a step in the right direction, it still suffers from the abstractness of the evaluation questions and that a non-creative system can still score high on the metrics.

5.3. Theory-based and Concrete

The work presented in paper III continues the ideology of theory driven evaluation as established earlier. For poem generation, a different theoretical approach, namely FACE was chosen. The theory defines creativity through framing, aesthetics, concepts and expressions. The main reason behind leaving the creative tripod behind and changing the theoretical framework was to see what might follow from a different theory in terms of computational modelling and evaluation. As it turned out, framing was an important aspect for solving abstractness in the evaluation questions.

In this section, I will discuss the framing and aesthetics evaluation presented in the paper as I consider it the most meaningful out of the evaluations. The evaluation of concepts was conducted automatically and the evaluation of expressions was a matter of preference between the master and the apprentice.

We used the notion of framing to fill a template of evaluation questions with the data provided by the master's fitness functions. These evaluation questions/ statements serve as a framing for the system to explain its creative decisions. The framing used for evaluation consisted of the following questions: *Do the words written in italics have rhymes (e.g. heikko peikko)?, Do the words written in italics have assonance (e.g. talo sano)?, Do the words written in italics have consonance (e.g. sakko sokka)?* and *Does the poem have alliteration within a verse (e.g. vanha vesi)?*. And the following statements: *Verse number X and Y have the same meter, The poem has X semantic fields: [semantic cluster 1]... and [semantic cluster N], The semantic fields [semantic cluster X] and [semantic cluster Y] are the closest to each other, The semantic fields [semantic cluster A] and [semantic cluster B] are the furthest away from each other, The following words in the poem [concrete words] are concrete concepts, The verse number X is positive, The verse number Y is negative, The following words in the poem [metaphorical words] can be understood metaphorically* and *The word X has a metaphorical connection to word Y*. The system would mark all rhyming words of any kind with italics and fill in the placeholders in the evaluation statements with the fitness functions.

As a difference to the previous papers, we did not use a 5-point Likert scale in this evaluation. Instead, we gave people three options: agree, disagree and I don't know. The reason behind this is simple, it is easier to interpret what it means when people either agree or disagree than if people showed an average agreement of 3.25 on one system versus 3.31 on another, which was one of the problems of the evaluation presented in paper II. Also, this binary scaling removes some of the subjectivity that might arise from people using a Likert-scale. Having an option I don't know is also meant to reduce bias in the results. People are not forced to give an opinion, if they cannot clearly form one, which means that they are less likely to just pick one of the two options at mere random when they find the assessment difficult.

Again, the evaluation is targeted at the exact features that were modelled computationally in the fitness functions. But now, we are forcing the evaluation to concretely evaluate the output of the fitness functions. If, for example a metaphor was predicted, we do not merely ask if the poem has a metaphor, which would be very open to interpretation; people might even understand something metaphorically the system was not aware of during the creative process. But we give a listing of the predicted metaphorical words and even an example of a metaphorical interpretation by the machine. This reduces the high level of subjectivity typically involved in CC evaluation even further by giving less room for interpretation.

The results obtained this way are more revealing of the shortcoming of the system than in the previously presented papers I and II. Even though rhyming is measured by rule-based metrics that work well for a language like Finnish that has a highly phonetic writing system, none of the rhyming questions received a 100% agreement by people and the fitness functions. In fact, we can indeed find a shortcoming in the fitness functions based on this evaluation. While they do measure the presence of the different types of rhyming correctly, they do not measure their quality. This means, for instance, that words such as *en* (I don't) and *et* (you don't) would be rated as having assonance by the system as they fill the main criterion: two different words that share the same vowels but have different consonants. However, such an assonance is hardly perceivable by people. This indicates that in the future, the system should measure rhyming by some metric more nuanced than just its mere existence in the poem. Consonance rhyme scored particularly lowly, which is mostly due to the fact that it is not the most typical type of rhyming in Finnish poetry and people are unfamiliar with it.

The statements relating to semantic clusters received the highest number of I don't know answers from the judges, this was also the case for the last statement about metaphors. This result, even though it does not really help in gaining knowledge about the performance of the method on these aspects, is still useful. It highlights that the questions of this kind, while being very important for poetry, are still difficult for people to assess when asked this concretely. This raises the question what the abstract evaluation questions that are typically used really measure, how can we feel any confidence about the results of a questionnaire assessing metaphoricity of a poem in a 5-point Likert scale using an abstract question, when people tend not to know when the question is asked more concretely? The results for the penultimate evaluation statement of metaphoricity showed relatively high agreement and lower number of I don't know answers. However, this statement leaves more room for interpretation than the last one.

For sentiment analysis, the method used clearly excelled in predicting positive sentiment, but did not work nearly as well for negative sentiment. Perhaps this is due to the fact that sentiment in poetry is conveyed and understood very differently than in regular language. For instance, *autumn leaves are falling,* is neither negative nor positive on a surface level, yet in a poem it might convey the idea of death or an end of an era of joy and happiness.

All in all, we can say that this evaluation method shows more clearly the problems of the system and gives some exact ideas for improvement such as the quality of rhymes and a sentiment analysis that caters more to sentiment in poetry in particular. As for the statements receiving a high number of I don't know answers, a more qualitative approach could be taken in the future in evaluating them. Or perhaps their nature is such that these questions can better be assessed by experts in poetry than ordinary people.

6. CONCLUSIONS AND FUTURE WORK

The contributions of this thesis reach to all of the three important components of computational creativity: theory, practice and evaluation. Paying attention to all of the three instead of only one alone has made it possible for symbiosis between the three components, which I believe to be vital for any work aiming to build computationally creative systems. Theoretical definitions are needed to narrow down and properly describe the problem one seeks to solve by computational means; they are important for motivating creativity in the proposed practical solution and ultimately for formulating the evaluation of the system. Without a definition for the problem one seeks to model, it is impossible to tell the degree to which the problem has been solved by the proposed solution. This type of practice without clear definitions will doom the field to not advancing from a stage where new models can be proposed easily, but their intercomparison is difficult and progress is not measurable.

From the theoretical perspective, in this thesis, I have presented a definition for generating movie title puns and Finnish poetry, both of them are based on different higher-level theories of computational creativity. It is important to note that the resulting definitions are not the only possible ones, and especially, in the case of poetry, the definition was not meant to define the ever-changing genre of poetry as a whole, but rather it was to narrow it down to something that can be computationally modelled.

The larger theoretical contribution of my thesis was the elaboration of a theoretical framework of my own. My theory, unlike the existing ones on computational creativity, explicitly states the need for meaning. People do not use language exclusively to evoke a certain emotional response or exhibit artistic value by their wording. Words are used to convey a concrete meaning, and this should also be considered in future research aiming to generate creative language. However, this is a difficult task indeed and the practical applications of this thesis have merely focused on the aesthetic rather than the communicative. This would, however, be an interesting line of work which I will be heading towards in the future.

From the practical point of view to computational creativity, we have elaborated a master-apprentice approach. The genetic algorithm, the master, serves an important role in making it possible to model the individually important aspects of computational creativity as defined from a theoretical point of view. A genetic algorithm also makes it possible to have diversity in the output due to the randomness introduced by the genetic process itself. This is particularly useful and desirable behaviour in a creative system. The NMT model, the apprentice, makes it possible to approximate autonomous creativity, and it gives us some intriguing information how human authored data affects the results when perceived by people.

The tale of the master and the apprentice is far from over. Currently, we are interested in taking the approach more towards the direction of a proper multi-agent system. This opens up a great deal of new research questions one can study in such a setting. Such as how would learning from very distinctive masters affect the results of the apprentice, or what if masters could learn from apprentices or apprentices from one another. The approach could be also tried out in contexts outside of the computational creativity domain to see if using a genetic algorithm to generate training data in a resource poor scenario has a positive impact when training an LSTM model.

Evaluation has been of particular interest throughout the work presented in this thesis. Evaluation should be conducted in such a way that it evaluates the individual aspects that have been computationally modelled. A system scoring high on a metric it was not aware of can hardly do so because of its own merit, but rather because people are willing to read more into its output than what the system ever intended. Furthermore, the evaluation becomes more useful in pointing out the merits and shortcomings of the system if it is done with as concrete evaluation questions as possible. Abstract questions leave too much room for interpretation making it more difficult to say whether the measured feature was the one the system intended or if the evaluators read more into the output.

Nevertheless, evaluation is a question far from solved despite the findings presented in this thesis. It is still an open question the degree to which one should rely on amateurs and experts in the evaluation process. The evaluation process itself is also something that should be more carefully studied in the future. In our evaluations, we have always shuffled the order of the artefacts so that there would be as little a constant priming effect as possible and we have been careful in not revealing to the judges they are evaluating computer generated artefacts. However, not all papers conduct the evaluation in this manner. In the future, it would be important to see whether shuffling or not and revealing that the artefacts are generated by a computer or not has a real measurable effect on the evaluation results.

During the process of my doctoral research, I have also published several open-source Python libraries relating to NLG that people can use freely. These are UralicNLP[3], Syntaxmaker[4] (described in paper VI), FinMeter[5] (the aesthetics of paper III) and Murre[6] (described in paper V). All of these are also permanently archived on Zenodo with a new DOI for every new release.

---

[3] https://github.com/mikahama/uralicNLP
[4] https://github.com/mikahama/syntaxmaker
[5] https://github.com/mikahama/finmeter
[6] https://github.com/mikahama/murre

REFERENCES

Aggarwal, S., & Mamidi, R. (2017). Automatic generation of jokes in Hindi. In *Proceedings of ACL 2017, Student Research Workshop* (pp. 69-74).

Alnajjar, K (2019). Computational Analysis and Generation of Slogans. Master's Thesis. *University of Helsinki, Faculty of Science*

Alnajjar, K., & Hämäläinen, M. (2018). A master-apprentice approach to automatic creation of culturally satirical movie titles. In *Proceedings of the 11th International Conference on Natural Language Generation* (pp. 274-283).

Asmis, E. (1992). Plato on poetic creativity. In R. Kraut (Ed.), *The Cambridge Companion to Plato* (Cambridge Companions to Philosophy, pp. 338-364). Cambridge: Cambridge University Press. doi:10.1017/CCOL0521430186.01

Attardo, S., & Raskin, V. (1991). Script theory revis (it) ed: Joke similarity and joke representation model. *Humor-International Journal of Humor Research*, 4(3-4), 293-348.

Baumrind, D. (1991). Parenting styles and adolescent development. *The Encyclopedia of Adolescence* (pp. 758–772).

Bedworth, J., & Norwood, J. (1999). The Turing test is dead.... In *Proceedings of the 3rd Conference on Creativity & Cognition* (pp. 193-194).

Bertero, D., & Fung, P. (2016). Deep learning of audio and language features for humor prediction. In *Proceedings of the Tenth International Conference on Language Resources and Evaluation (LREC'16)* (pp. 496-501).

Boden, M. A. (2004). The creative mind: Myths and mechanisms. Routledge.

Brownell, H. H., Michel, D., Powelson, J., & Gardner, H. (1983). Surprise but not coherence: Sensitivity to verbal humor in right-hemisphere patients. *Brain and language*, 18(1), 20-27.

Burroway, J. (2007). Imaginative writing: The elements of craft. *Longman Pub Group*.

Caccavale, F., & Søgaard, A. (2019). Predicting Concrete and Abstract Entities in Modern Poetry. In *Proceedings of the AAAI Conference on Artificial Intelligence* (Vol. 33, pp. 858-864).

Chalmers, D. J. (1995). Absent qualia, fading qualia, dancing qualia. *Conscious experience*, 309-328.

Chen, P. Y., & Soo, V. W. (2018). Humor recognition using deep learning. In *Proceedings of the 2018 Conference of the North American Chapter of the Association for Computational Linguistics: Human Language Technologies, Volume 2 (Short Papers)* (pp. 113-117).

Chikai, K., Takayama, J., & Arase, Y. (2019). Responsive and Self-Expressive Dialogue Generation. In *Proceedings of the First Workshop on NLP for Conversational AI* (pp. 139-149).

Colton, S. (2008). Creativity Versus the Perception of Creativity in Computational Systems. In *AAAI spring symposium: creative intelligent systems* (Vol. 8).

Colton, S., Charnley, J. W., & Pease, A. (2011). Computational Creativity Theory: The FACE and IDEA Descriptive Models. In *The 2nd International Conference on Computational Creativity* (pp. 90-95).

Colton, S., & Wiggins, G. A. (2012). Computational creativity: the final frontier?. In *Proceedings of the 20th European Conference on Artificial Intelligence* (pp. 21-26).

Cook, M., Colton, S., Pease, A., & Llano, M. T. (2019). Framing in computational creativity–a survey and taxonomy. In *Proceedings of the 10th International Conference on Computational Creativity* (pp. 156-163).

Davis, N. M. (2013). Human-computer co-creativity: Blending human and computational creativity. In *Ninth Artificial Intelligence and Interactive Digital Entertainment Conference*.

Deb, K., Pratap, A., Agarwal, S., & Meyarivan, T. A. M. T. (2002). A fast and elitist multiobjective genetic algorithm: NSGA-II. *IEEE transactions on evolutionary computation*, 6(2), 182-197.

Feng, Y., & Wan, X. (2019). Learning Bilingual Sentiment-Specific Word Embeddings without Cross-lingual Supervision. In *Proceedings of the 2019 Conference of the North American Chapter of the Association for Computational Linguistics: Human Language Technologies, Volume 1 (Long and Short Papers)* (pp. 420-429).

Fortin, F. A., Rainville, F. M. D., Gardner, M. A., Parizeau, M., & Gagné, C. (2012). DEAP: Evolutionary algorithms made easy. *Journal of Machine Learning Research*, 13(Jul), (pp. 2171-2175).

Frey, B. J., & Dueck, D. (2007). Clustering by passing messages between data points. *Science*, 315(5814), 972-976.

Gaut, B. (2012). Creativity and Rationality. *The Journal of Aesthetics and Art Criticism*, 70(3), (pp. 259-270). www.jstor.org/stable/43496511

Gervás, P. (2018). Targeted Storyfying: Creating Stories About Particular Events. In *the Proceedings of the 9th International Conference on Computational Creativity* (pp. 232-239).

Gervás, P. (2017). Template-Free Construction of Poems with Thematic Cohesion and Enjambment. In *Proceedings of the Workshop on Computational Creativity in Natural Language Generation (CC-NLG 2017)* (pp. 21-28).

Goffman, E. (1959) The Presentation of Self in Everyday Life. *University of Edinburgh Social Sciences Research Centre*

Grice, H. P. (1975). Logic and conversation. In *Speech acts* (pp. 41-58). Brill.

He, H., Peng, N., & Liang, P. (2019). Pun Generation with Surprise. In *Proceedings of the 2019 Conference of the North American Chapter of the Association for Computational Linguistics: Human Language Technologies, Volume 1 (Long and Short Papers)* (pp. 1734-1744).

Hennessey, B. A., & Amabile, T. (2010) Creativity. *Annual Review of Psychology*, 61(1), (pp. 569-598).

Honkela, T. (2017). Rauhankone: tekoälytutkijan testamentti. *Gaudeamus*.

Hossain, N., Krumm, J., & Gamon, M. (2019). "President Vows to Cut< Taxes> Hair": Dataset and Analysis of Creative Text Editing for Humorous Headlines. In *Proceedings of the 2019 Conference of the North American Chapter of the Association for Computational Linguistics: Human Language Technologies, Volume 1 (Long and Short Papers)* (pp. 133-142).

Hämäläinen, M. (2018). Harnessing NLG to Create Finnish Poetry Automatically. In the Proceedings of the 9th International Conference on Computational Creativity (pp. 9-15). Association for Computational Creativity (ACC).

Hämäläinen, M. (2019). UralicNLP: An NLP library for Uralic languages. *Journal of Open Source Software*, 4(37), 1345.

Hämäläinen, M., & Alnajjar, K. (2019). Creative contextual dialog adaptation in an open world RPG. In *Proceedings of the 14th International Conference on the Foundations of Digital Games*.

Jennings, K. E. (2010). Developing creativity: Artificial barriers in artificial intelligence. *Minds and Machines*, 20(4), (pp. 489-501).

Jordanous, A. (2012). A standardised procedure for evaluating creative systems: Computational creativity evaluation based on what it is to be creative. *Cognitive Computation*, 4(3), (pp. 246-279).

Kantokorpi, M., Viikari, A., & Lyytikäinen, P. (1990). Runousopin perusteet. *Gaudeamus*.

Kao, J., & Jurafsky, D. (2012). A computational analysis of style, affect, and imagery in contemporary poetry. In *Proceedings of the NAACL-HLT 2012 workshop on computational linguistics for literature* (pp. 8-17).

Kim, J. (2018). Philosophy of mind. *Routledge*.

Klein, G., Kim, Y., Deng, Y., Nguyen, V., Senellart, J., & Rush, A. M. (2018). OpenNMT: Neural Machine Translation Toolkit. In *Proceedings of the 13th Conference of the Association for Machine Translation in the Americas (Volume 1: Research Papers)* (pp. 177-184).

Lau, J. H., Cohn, T., Baldwin, T., Brooke, J., & Hammond, A. (2018). Deep-speare: A joint neural model of poetic language, meter and rhyme. In *Proceedings of the 56th Annual Meeting of the Association for Computational Linguistics (Volume 1: Long Papers)* (pp. 1948-1958).

Lamb, C., Brown, D. G., & Clarke, C. L. (2018). Evaluating computational creativity: An interdisciplinary tutorial. *ACM Computing Surveys (CSUR)*, 51(2), (pp. 1-34).

Lamb, C., Brown, D. G., & Clarke, C. L. (2017). Incorporating novelty, meaning, reaction and craft into computational poetry: a negative experimental result. In *Proceedings of 8th International Conference on Computational Creativity* (pp. 183-188).

Loller-Andersen, M., & Gambäck, B. (2018). Deep Learning-based Poetry Generation Given Visual Input. In *the Proceedings of the 9th International Conference on Computational Creativity* (pp. 240-247).

Lotman, J. M., (1974). Den poetiska texten. *Stockholm.*

Lubart, T. (2005). How can computers be partners in the creative process: classification and commentary on the special issue. *International Journal of Human-Computer Studies*, 63(4-5), (pp. 365-369).

Luo, F., Li, S., Yang, P., Li, L., Chang, B., Sui, Z., & Xu, S. U. N. (2019, November). Pun-GAN: Generative Adversarial Network for Pun Generation. In *Proceedings of the 2019 Conference on Empirical Methods in Natural Language Processing and the 9th International Joint Conference on Natural Language Processing (EMNLP-IJCNLP)* (pp. 3379-3384).

Manurung, R., Ritchie, G., & Thompson, H. (2012). Using genetic algorithms to create meaningful poetic text. *Journal of Experimental & Theoretical Artificial Intelligence*, 24(1), 43-64.

Marsella, S., Gratch, J., & Petta, P. (2010). Computational models of emotion. *A Blueprint for Affective Computing-A sourcebook and manual*, 11(1), 21-46.

McCharty, J. (2007) What is artificial intelligence? Technical report, Computer Science Department, Stanford University

Gonçalo Oliveira, H., (2017). A survey on intelligent poetry generation: Languages, features, techniques, reutilisation and evaluation. In *Proceedings of the 10th International Conference on Natural Language Generation* (pp. 11-20).

Gonçalo Oliveira, H., & Alves, A. O. (2016). Poetry from concept maps–yet another adaptation of PoeTryMe's flexible architecture. In *Proceedings of 7th International Conference on Computational Creativity, ICCC.* (pp. 246-253)

Gonçalo Oliveira, H., Costa, D., & Pinto, A. M. (2016). One does not simply produce funny memes! – explorations on the automatic generation of internet humor. In *Proceedings of the Seventh International Conference on Computational Creativity (ICCC 2016).* (pp. 238-245).

Oring, E. (2003). Engaging humor. *University of Illinois Press.*

Pease, A., & Colton, S. (2011). On impact and evaluation in computational creativity: A discussion of the Turing test and an alternative proposal. In Proceedings of the AISB symposium on AI and Philosophy (Vol. 39).

Pirinen, T. A. (2015). Development and Use of Computational Morphology of Finnish in the Open Source and Open Science Era: Notes on Experiences with Omorfi Development. SKY Journal of Linguistics, 28. (pp. 381-393).

Pollak, S., Boshkoska, B. M., Miljkovic, D., Wiggins, G. A., & Lavrac, N. (2016). Computational creativity conceptualisation grounded on ICCC papers. In *Proceedings of the Seventh International Conference on Computational Creativity*. (pp. 123-130)

Rahgozar, A., & Inkpen, D. (2019). Semantics and Homothetic Clustering of Hafez Poetry. In *Proceedings of the 3rd Joint SIGHUM Workshop on Computational Linguistics for Cultural Heritage, Social Sciences, Humanities and Literature* (pp. 82-90).

Raskin, V. (1985). Semantic mechanisms of humor (Vol. 24). *Springer Science & Business Media*.

Reiter, E. (2018). A Structured Review of the Validity of BLEU. *Computational Linguistics*, 44(3), 393-401.

Rhodes, M. (1961). An analysis of creativity. *The Phi Delta Kappan*, 42(7), (pp. 305-310).

Richards, I. A. (1936). The philosophy of rhetoric. *Oxford University Press*

Searle, J. R. (1969). Speech acts: An essay in the philosophy of language (Vol. 626). *Cambridge university press*.

Shao Y, Zhang C, Zhou J, Gu T, Yuan Y. (2019) How Does Culture Shape Creativity? A Mini-Review. *Front Psychol*. 2019;10:1219. Published 2019 May 28. doi:10.3389/fpsyg.2019.01219

Shen X, Su H, Li Y, Li W, Niu S, Zhao Y, Aizawa A, Long G. A. (2017). Conditional Variational Framework for Dialog Generation. In *Proceedings of the 55th Annual Meeting of the Association for Computational Linguistics (Volume 2: Short Papers)* (pp. 504-509).

van Stegeren, J., & Theune, M. (2019). Churnalist: Fictional Headline Generation for Context-appropriate Flavor Text. In *10th International Conference on Computational Creativity* (pp. 65-72). Association for Computational Creativity.

Talman, A., & Chatzikyriakidis, S. (2019). Testing the Generalization Power of Neural Network Models across NLI Benchmarks. In *Proceedings of the 2019 ACL Workshop BlackboxNLP: Analyzing and Interpreting Neural Networks for NLP* (pp. 85-94).

Toral, A., Castilho, S., Hu, K., & Way, A. (2018). Attaining the Unattainable? Reassessing Claims of Human Parity in Neural Machine Translation. In *Proceedings of the Third Conference on Machine Translation: Research Papers* (pp. 113-123).

Veale, T. (2018) A Massive Sarcastic Robot: What a Great Idea! Two Approaches to the Computational Generation of Irony. In *the Proceedings of the 9th International Conference on Computational Creativity*. (pp. 120-127).

Veale, T. (2016). The shape of tweets to come: Automating language play in social networks. *Multiple Perspectives on Language Play*, 1, 73-92.

Veale, T. & Alnajjar, K. (2016) Grounded for life: creative symbol-grounding for lexical invention, *Connection Science*, 28:2, (pp. 139-154), DOI: 10.1080/09540091.2015.1130025

Wei, W., Le, Q., Dai, A., & Li, J. (2018). Airdialogue: An environment for goal-oriented dialogue research. In *Proceedings of the 2018 Conference on Empirical Methods in Natural Language Processing* (pp. 3844-3854).

Wiggins, G. A. (2006). A preliminary framework for description, analysis and comparison of creative systems. *Knowledge-Based Systems,* 19(7), (pp. 449-458).

Winters, T., Nys, V., & De Schreye, D. (2019). Towards a general framework for humor generation from rated examples. In *Proceedings of the 10th International Conference on Computational Creativity* (pp. 274-281).

Yang, D., Lavie, A., Dyer, C., & Hovy, E. (2015). Humor recognition and humor anchor extraction. In *Proceedings of the 2015 Conference on Empirical Methods in Natural Language Processing* (pp. 2367-2376).

Yang, Z., Cai, P., Feng, Y., Li, F., Feng, W., Chiu, E. S. Y., & Yu, H. (2019). Generating Classical Chinese Poems from Vernacular Chinese. In *Proceedings of the 2019 Conference on Empirical Methods in Natural Language Processing and the 9th International Joint Conference on Natural Language Processing (EMNLP-IJCNLP)* (pp. 6156-6165).

Yannakakis, G. N., Liapis, A., & Alexopoulos, C. (2014). Mixed-initiative co-creativity. In *Proceedings of the 9th Conference on the Foundations of Digital Games*.

Yi, X., Sun, M., Li, R., & Li, W. (2018). Automatic poetry generation with mutual reinforcement learning. In *Proceedings of the 2018 Conference on Empirical Methods in Natural Language Processing* (pp. 3143-3153).

Yu, Z., Tan, J., & Wan, X. (2018). A neural approach to pun generation. In *Proceedings of the 56th Annual Meeting of the Association for Computational Linguistics (Volume 1: Long Papers)* (pp. 1650-1660).

Zhang, J., Feng, Y., Wang, D., Wang, Y., Abel, A., Zhang, S., & Zhang, A. (2017). Flexible and Creative Chinese Poetry Generation Using Neural Memory. In *Proceedings of the 55th Annual Meeting of the Association for Computational Linguistics (Volume 1: Long Papers)* (pp. 1364-1373).

Generating Modern Poetry Automatically in Finnish

Mika Hämäläinen
Department of Digital Humanities
University of Helsinki
mika.hamalainen@helsinki.fi

Khalid Alnajjar
Department of Computer Science
University of Helsinki
khalid.alnajjar@helsinki.fi

Abstract

We present a novel approach for generating poetry automatically for the morphologically rich Finnish language by using a genetic algorithm. The approach improves the state of the art of the previous Finnish poem generators by introducing a higher degree of freedom in terms of structural creativity. Our approach is evaluated and described within the paradigm of computational creativity, where the fitness functions of the genetic algorithm are assimilated with the notion of aesthetics. The output is considered to be a poem 81.5% of the time by human evaluators.

1 Introduction

Poem generation is a challenging task for creative NLG (natural language generation) requiring structural integrity in the form of rhyming and meter, grammatical correctness and figurative expression. Poems are meant to be interpreted and therefore the meaning they convey cannot be fully explained by semantics, but they rather require an exploration into the notion of pragmatics.

In this paper, we present a novel approach based on a genetic algorithm for creating poetry in Finnish from the stand point of computational creativity. In addition to solving problems related to poems in general, the morphosyntactically complex Finnish sets additional requirements for producing grammatical output.

Computational creativity can be seen as a search for creative artefacts in a conceptual space (cf. Wiggins, 2006). Therefore the use of genetic algorithm for a creative task is reasonable as it conducts a search and picks out the most suitable candidates based on its fitness function. An important aspect for creativity is that the system should be able to assess its own creations, a notion called appreciation (Colton, 2008) or aesthetic function (Colton et al., 2011) in the literature. The fitness

function of the genetic algorithm serves for this exact purpose, as it can score the output in terms of different aesthetic dimensions.

2 Related work

In the past, poetry generation has been studied both from the point of view of computational creativity and natural language generation. Poem generation has been tackled with a variety of different methods such as case-based reasoning (Gervás, 2001), templates (Colton et al., 2012), translation with WFSTs (weighted finite-state transducers) (Greene et al., 2010), text transformation via word embeddings (Bay et al., 2017) and conditional variational autoencoders (Li et al., 2018). As the field of poem generation has been broadly discussed by Oliveira (2017), we dedicate the rest of this section to describing the existing poetry generation work conducted for Finnish within the computational creativity paradigm. We also discuss some previous approaches using genetic algorithms.

One of the first takes on Finnish poem generation is the P. O. Eticus system (Toivanen et al., 2012). P. O. Eticus uses a corpus of human authored poems. These poems are used as templates for generating new poetry. In practice, the system takes a random poem from the corpus, conducts a morphological analysis on it and replaces some of the words in the existing poem. The replaced words are inflected to match the morphology of the original word.

Another take on the poetry generation in Finnish is that of Kantosalo et al. (2015). This approach is presented as a part of a poem authoring system. How this generator operates is that it takes sentences form children's books stored in its corpus based on a shared keyword. These sentences serve as verses, or poem fragments, and

Proceedings of the 2019 Conference on Empirical Methods in Natural Language Processing
and the 9th International Joint Conference on Natural Language Processing, pages 6001–6006,
Hong Kong, China, November 3–7, 2019. ©2019 Association for Computational Linguistics

they are output one after another forming a generated poem. As the system does not alter text at all, it does not have to deal with the complexities of the Finnish morphology.

The most recent work on Finnish poem generation is the work presented by Hämäläinen (2018a). This approach consists of individual rule-based verse generators, each of which produces structurally different verses with different types of figurative expression, such as metaphors, tautology, comparison and so on. The verse generators are applied in the order defined by hand-written poem structures. Semantic cohesion is achieved by the fact that each verse generator outputs a noun to the following verse generator in the poem structure. This guarantees that verses are always coherent to some extent with the verse that immediately precedes them. This generator is in use in the creative internet application Poem Machine tailored for co-creativity (Hämäläinen, 2018b).

The previous approaches in Finnish poem generation covered in this section are limited in terms of structural creativity. The approaches are either limited by the structure imposed by the existing poems or sentences, or the hand-written verse structures. The approach we present in our paper showcases more creative freedom on the structural level. This, however, is challenging due to the complicated morphosyntax of Finnish; structural changes can easily render the results nonsensical as wrong morphology in an incorrect syntactic position will make the entire sentence nongrammatical. We take this into account in our proposed method.

Genetic algorithms have been used in the generation of poetic language before. Although not full poem generation, Hervás et al. (2007) have used genetic algorithms for generating alliterations in Spanish. In terms of full poetry generation, Manurung et al. (2012) aim for *grammaticality*, *meaningfulness* and *poeticness* with their genetic algorithm approach. Their approach tires to maximize the similarity of the poem meter to the target meter, and the poem semantics to the target semantics, while still retaining grammaticality.

A recent approach to poem generation with genetic algorithms, TwitSong 3.0 (Lamb and Brown, 2019), is based on a mined corpus of sentences that are used as verses in poems based on their inter-compatibility in terms of rhyming. They base their fitness functions on the following met-

rics: (*meter, emotion, topicality* and *imagery*). The fitness functions operate on verse level. They solve emotion and imagery with existing lexicons, topicality is assessed based on trigram and keyword similarity with the desired topic and meter is scored based on how close it is to a iambic meter.

3 Poem Generator

This section is dedicated to describing the data used for poem generation, the genetic algorithm and how the Finnish morphosyntax is solved by the system. Special attention is paid to describing the fitness functions, according to which the system can rank its creations.

3.1 Data

We crawl Wikisources[1] for Finnish poetry. This way we obtain 6,189 poems. We parse the poems by using the Finnish dependency parser (Haverinen et al., 2014) to obtain syntactic relations, morphological features, part of speech and lemma for each word. This constitutes our poem corpus, denoted as P, with verse-level syntactic parsing. These poems are used by the genetic algorithm for the initial population, where a stanza of a human authored poem is treated as one poem.

For semantics, we use the pretrained word2vec word embeddings[2] trained on the Finnish Internet Parsebank (Kanerva et al., 2014). This word2vec model has been trained on lemmatized data, which is important as we are interested in obtaining replacement words in an uninflected form.

3.2 Genetic Algorithm

Genetic algorithms are inspired by evolution taking place in the real world. They have an initial set of individuals forming a population. These individuals are then exposed to evolutionary processes such as mutation and crossover. After a generation, the fittest individuals survive to the next generation and the evolutionary process is repeated. For modeling this process, we use the Python library DEAP (Fortin et al., 2012) as the genetic algorithms framework.

We employ a standard $(\mu + \lambda)$ genetic algorithm, which has previously been used in computational creativity applications (see Alnajjar et al.,

---

[1]https://fi.wikisource.org
[2]http://bionlp-www.utu.fi/fin-vector-space-models/fin-word2vec-lemma.bin

2018). The method begins by constructing an initial population and then evolving it, while optimizing certain parameters, throughout G generations. At each generation step, the fittest μ individuals in the current population and the λ offspring are selected to represent the next population. We empirically set μ and λ to 100 and G to 25. Additionally, the algorithm takes two user-defined inputs, a poem p and a theme t. For our case, we considered a theme t as a single word representing an abstract concept such as *nature*; alternatively, a set of words could be used instead to represent a more focused theme (e.g. *tree*, *forest*, *flower*, ... etc).

3.2.1 Initial Population

To build an initial population containing poems with various syntactic structures, the method makes μ copies of the input poem p. For each poem, the method then replaces one verse in it with a random verse from a different poem existing in the poem corpus P.

3.2.2 Mutation and Crossover

In our method, we implement one type of mutation which selects a random content word in the poem. The term content word in this case refers to a word that belongs to an open class part-of-speech category. The selected word is substituted with another semantically similar word, which is determined as follows. Let w be the random content word selected to be replaced, the method retrieves the top 300 semantically similar words to w as candidate replacements from the word2vec model. Thereafter, the method uses UralicNLP (Hämäläinen, 2019) to perform morphological analysis on all candidate words. The candidate words that have a different part-of-speech tag than the original word w are omitted out. Out of the remaining candidate words, a random word is picked to substitute w.

We use a single-point crossover at the verse-level. In practice, this means that during the evolutionary process two poem individuals are selected and a single point at the beginning of their verses is chosen at random. Verses after that point are swapped between them.

3.2.3 Fitness Functions

The genetic algorithm assesses the individuals based on six metrics that evaluate the poem's structure and one metric that evaluates semantics. The difference in the number of syllables in verses and in the poetic foot, as measured by the distribution of long and short syllables, are contrasted to the original poem. The genetic algorithm is set to minimize these values to keep the difference minimal. As not changing the poem at all would result in the minimum difference in these values, we penalize identical verses by giving them a distance of 20. This way the genetic algorithm tries to make changes so that results following the original meter are preferred.

The number of full rhymes, assonance rhymes and consonance rhymes in between the verses of each generated poem are used as metrics to assess to overall poetic quality of the individuals. The number of alliterating words is counted within verses as this type of rhyme is traditionally occurring within verses in Finnish poetry. The values given by these four metrics are maximized by the genetic algorithm to get the maximum number rhyming words in the final outputs.

The last metric measures the average semantic similarity of the words in the poem to the input theme t with the word2vec model. Maximizing this function pushes the evolutionary process towards creating poems that are close in semantics to the desired input theme.

As we are employing multiple objective functions in our genetic algorithm, we resort to using a non-dominant sorting algorithm (NSGA-II) (Deb et al., 2002) for optimizing these functions. In short, the algorithm selects individuals that are not dominated by any other individual. An individual x is considered to be dominating another if its scores on all objective functions are greater than or equal to y's and it is always better than y on at least one objective.

3.3 Surface Generation

As the genetic algorithm does substitutions on the level of lemmas, it is important to be able to turn the verses with new lemmas into grammatical sentences. This is not only needed for presenting the final output produced by the genetic algorithm to people, but also for the fitness functions to work.

In Finnish, the surface form of a word (morphological realization) is affected by two mechanisms: agreement and government. The former means that certain words have to share morphological features in a sentence. For example, adjectives will have to follow the case and number of the noun they modify, like so: *punainen talo* (a red house) and *punaisessa talossa* (in a red house). This can be accounted for just by inflecting the replacement word with the morphology of the original word. For this purpose we use Omorfi (Pirinen et al., 2017) which implements Finnish morphology as an FST (finite-state transducer).

Government, on the other hand, requires some additional work. In government, words affect on each other morphologically in a way that depends on the governor. This means that if a governor word is replaced by another one in the sentence, the morphology of the governed word needs to adapt to the change. In concrete, given an original verse *uneksin hatusta* (I dream of a hat) and a change of the verb to *näen hatun* (I see a hat), the case of the object for *hattu* has to change from elative to genitive. We resolve government with Syntax maker (Hämäläinen and Rueter, 2018), which resolves the required case based on corpus statistics.

4 Results and Evaluation

As evaluation of creative systems is one of the most difficult problems in the field of computational creativity, instead of trying to come up with an evaluation metric of our own, we opt for the evaluation method used to evaluate a previous Finnish poem generator. In practice, this means conducting a quantitative evaluation with human judges with the evaluation questions defined by Toivanen et al. (2012).

An additional reasoning for using human evaluators instead of automated evaluation metrics is the poor correlation observed in a previous study (Hämäläinen and Alnajjar, 2019) of automatic evaluation metrics such as BLEU (Papineni et al., 2002) and PINC (Chen and Dolan, 2011) scores with human judgments when evaluating creativity of a system.

We run the genetic algorithm to produce a final population for 20 different initial poems for four different themes *luonto* (nature), *perhe* (family), *lemmikki* (pet) and *ihminen* (human). From each of the 20 final populations, we pick one poem at random. We shuffle the order of poems to reduce the priming effect of poems appearing always in a given order. We divide the 20 poems into two batches of 10 poems to reduce the effort of an individual evaluator. Each batch of 10 is then evaluated by 10 different human evaluators recruited from the university campus. The total number

of evaluators is 20 and all of them are native in Finnish.

We use the following evaluation questions from Toivanen et al. (2012): (1) *How typical is the text as a poem?* (2) *How understandable is it?* (3) *How good is the language?* (4) *Does the text evoke mental images?* (5) *Does the text evoke emotions?* (6) *How much do you like the text?.* These questions are evaluated in a 5 point Likert scale, where 1 represents the worst and 5 the best grade. In addition to these questions, one simple binary question is asked: *Is the text a poem?.*

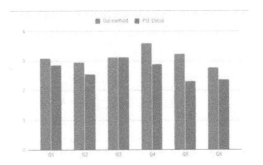

Figure 1: Evaluation results

Figure 1 represents the average values of the results of the human evaluation for each question. The plot also shows the evaluation results of P.O. Eticus as obtained in their study. As we can see, our method shows higher ratings on all the evaluation questions except for question 3. As for the binary question, the judges rated the output as a poem 81.5% of the time which is exactly the same result as P.O. Eticus got.

However, it is to remember that as a high level of subjectivity is involved in this evaluation setting, our results should not be directly compared to those of P.O. Eticus. The results form their study should taken more as a reference, rather than a definite proof that our system always outperforms P.O. Eticus.

	Q1	Q2	Q3	Q4	Q5	Q6
Average	3.10	2.94	3.11	3.60	3.23	2.77
Median	3	3	3	4	3	3
Mode	2	2	3	4	4	2

Table 1: The average, median and mode of the evaluation results

Table 1 shows the median and mode of the results in addition to the average values. The median values seems to correspond to the rounded average values. However, the mode deviates in the case of the first, second, fifth and last questions as the most chosen answer by the judges was different from the average.

> *Ja kultaa, kuninkaankin saan.*
> *Ja laulut ne kiertävät maata ja merta*
> *Jos virkkaan kun orja*
> *Aina, todella Herra pahankurisuutta antaa.*

> And gold, of a king I shall have.
> And songs, they shall roam on the land and the sea
> If I knit like a slave
> Always, indeed the Lord shall wrack his mischief.

Above is an example of a poem generated by the system and its translation in English. The poems generated by the system are typically of this length as the genetic algorithm uses a stanza of an existing poem as its starting point.

5 Discussion and Conclusion

The method presented in this paper shows improvement on a previously used evaluation metric. However, based on the discussions we had with some of the human evaluators after they had given their judgment, it became evident that people have very different criteria for poetry. Some of the judges had guessed that they were reading computer generated poems, even though this detail was not revealed to them explicitly. Their judgments were the most critical towards the generated poetry. On the other hand, the evaluators, who were struck by a surprise that the poems were generated by a computer, were in general more generous in their judgments. One of the evaluators almost refused to believe the poems were generated by a computer instead of a person.

The high level of subjectivity that we could observe just by talking with people calls for a more robust qualitative study on the poem evaluation problem itself in the future. This would allow us to uncover additional factors that affect on the judgments given by people. Furthermore, conducting a study just on the evaluation itself makes it possible for us to evaluate the adequacy of the used evaluation metric in evaluating computer generated poetry.

Nevertheless, the scores achieved by our system, in relation to a previous method by following the same evaluation metric, are promising as they are indicative of potentially higher quality in the output. We have presented a solution for the Finnish morphosyntax in conjunction with employing a genetic algorithm to cater for computational creativity in poem generation.

Acknowledgements

Special thanks to Jack Rueter for helping out with the evaluation.

References

Khalid Alnajjar, Hadaytullah Hadaytullah, and Hannu Toivonen. 2018. "Talent, Skill and Support." A method for automatic creation of slogans. In *Proceedings of the 9th International Conference on Computational Creativity (ICCC 2018)*, pages 88–95, Salamanca, Spain. Association for Computational Creativity.

Benjamin Bay, Paul Bodily, and Dan Ventura. 2017. Text transformation via constraints and word embedding. In *Proceedings of the Eighth International Conference on Computational Creativity*, pages 49–56.

David L Chen and William B Dolan. 2011. Collecting highly parallel data for paraphrase evaluation. In *Proceedings of the 49th Annual Meeting of the Association for Computational Linguistics: Human Language Technologies-Volume 1*, pages 190–200.

Simon Colton. 2008. Creativity Versus the Perception of Creativity in Computational Systems. In *AAAI Spring Symposium: Creative Intelligent Systems*, Technical Report SS-08-03, pages 14—20, Stanford, California, USA.

Simon Colton, John William Charnley, and Alison Pease. 2011. Computational creativity theory: The face and idea descriptive models. In *ICCC*, pages 90–95.

Simon Colton, Jacob Goodwin, and Tony Veale. 2012. Full-face poetry generation. In *Proceedings of the Third International Conference on Computational Creativity*, pages 95—102.

K. Deb, A. Pratap, S. Agarwal, and T. Meyarivan. 2002. A fast and elitist multiobjective genetic algorithm: Nsga-ii. *IEEE Transactions on Evolutionary Computation*, 6(2):182–197.

Félix-Antoine Fortin, François-Michel De Rainville, Marc-André Gardner, Marc Parizeau, and Christian Gagné. 2012. DEAP: Evolutionary algorithms made easy. *Journal of Machine Learning Research*, 13:2171–2175.

Pablo Gervás. 2001. An expert system for the composition of formal Spanish poetry. *Knowledge-Based Systems*, 14(3):181–188.

Erica Greene, Tugba Bodrumlu, and Kevin Knight. 2010. Automatic analysis of rhythmic poetry with applications to generation and translation. In *Proceedings of the 2010 Conference on Empirical Methods in Natural Language Processing*, EMNLP '10, pages 524–533, Stroudsburg, PA, USA. Association for Computational Linguistics.

Mika Hämäläinen. 2018a. Harnessing NLG to Create Finnish Poetry Automatically. In *Proceedings of the Ninth International Conference on Computational Creativity*, pages 9–15.

Mika Hämäläinen. 2018b. Poem Machine - a Co-creative NLG Web Application for Poem Writing. In *The 11th International Conference on Natural Language Generation: Proceedings of the Conference*, pages 195—196.

Mika Hämäläinen. 2019. UralicNLP: An NLP library for Uralic languages. *Journal of Open Source Software*, 4(37):1345.

Mika Hämäläinen and Khalid Alnajjar. 2019. Modelling the Socialization of Creative Agents in a Master-Apprentice Setting: The Case of Movie Title Puns. In *Proceedings of the Tenth International Conference on Computational Creativity*, pages 266–273.

Mika Hämäläinen and Jack Rueter. 2018. Development of an Open Source Natural Language Generation Tool for Finnish. In *Proceedings of the Fourth International Workshop on Computational Linguistics for Uralic Languages*, pages 51–58.

Katri Haverinen, Jenna Nyblom, Timo Viljanen, Veronika Laippala, Samuel Kohonen, Anna Missilä, Stina Ojala, Tapio Salakoski, and Filip Ginter. 2014. Building the essential resources for finnish: the turku dependency treebank. *Language Resources and Evaluation*, 48(3):493–531.

Raquel Hervás, Jason Robinson, and Pablo Gervás. 2007. Evolutionary assistance in alliteration and allelic drivel. In *Workshops on Applications of Evolutionary Computation*, pages 537–546. Springer.

Jenna Kanerva, Juhani Luotolahti, Veronika Laippala, and Filip Ginter. 2014. Syntactic n-gram collection from a large-scale corpus of internet Finnish. In *Human Language Technologies-The Baltic Perspective: Proceedings of the Sixth International Conference Baltic HLT*, volume 268, pages 184–191.

Anna Kantosalo, Jukka Toivanen, and Hannu Toivonen. 2015. Interaction Evaluation for Human-Computer Co-creativity: A Case Study. In *Proceedings of the Sixth International Conference on Computational Creativity*, pages 276–283.

Carolyn Lamb and Daniel G. Brown. 2019. Twit-Song 3.0: towards semantic revisions in computational poetry. In *Proceedings of the Tenth International Conference on Computational Creativity*, pages 212–219.

Juntao Li, Yan Song, Haisong Zhang, Dongmin Chen, Shuming Shi, Dongyan Zhao, and Rui Yan. 2018. Generating classical Chinese poems via conditional variational autoencoder and adversarial training. In *Proceedings of the 2018 Conference on Empirical Methods in Natural Language Processing*, pages 3890–3900, Brussels, Belgium. Association for Computational Linguistics.

Ruli Manurung, Graeme Ritchie, and Henry Thompson. 2012. Using genetic algorithms to create meaningful poetic text. *J. Exp. Theor. Artif. Intell.*, 24:43–64.

Hugo Gonçalo Oliveira. 2017. A survey on intelligent poetry generation: Languages, features, techniques, reutilisation and evaluation. In *Proceedings of the 10th International Conference on Natural Language Generation*, pages 11–20, Santiago de Compostela, Spain. Association for Computational Linguistics.

Kishore Papineni, Salim Roukos, Todd Ward, and Wei-Jing Zhu. 2002. Bleu: a method for automatic evaluation of machine translation. In *Proceedings of the 40th annual meeting on association for computational linguistics*, pages 311–318.

Tommi A Pirinen, Inari Listenmaa, Ryan Johnson, Francis M. Tyers, and Juha Kuokkala. 2017. Open morphology of finnish. LINDAT/CLARIN digital library at the Institute of Formal and Applied Linguistics, Charles University.

Jukka Toivanen, Hannu Toivonen, Alessandro Valitutti, and Oskar Gross. 2012. Corpus-Based Generation of Content and Form in Poetry. In *Proceedings of the Third International Conference on Computational Creativity*.

Geraint A Wiggins. 2006. A preliminary framework for description, analysis and comparison of creative systems. *Knowledge-Based Systems*, 19(7):449–458.

Modelling the Socialization of Creative Agents in a Master-Apprentice Setting: The Case of Movie Title Puns

Mika Hämäläinen
Department of Digital Humanities
Faculty of Arts
University of Helsinki
mika.hamalainen@helsinki.fi

Khalid Alnajjar
Department of Computer Science
Faculty of Science
University of Helsinki
alnajjar@cs.helsinki.fi

Abstract

This paper presents work on modelling the social psychological aspect of socialization in the case of a computationally creative master-apprentice system. In each master-apprentice pair, the master, a genetic algorithm, is seen as a parent for its apprentice, which is an NMT based sequence-to-sequence model. The effect of different parenting styles on the creative output of each pair is in the focus of this study. This approach brings a novel view point to computational social creativity, which has mainly focused in the past on computationally creative agents being on a socially equal level, whereas our approach studies the phenomenon in the context of a social hierarchy.

Introduction

The master-apprentice approach, as introduced by (Alnajjar and Hämäläinen 2018), to computational creativity has been shown to achieve creative autonomy and its creativity has been thoroughly discussed and motivated. However, the question that has remained without an answer has been the social nature of a master-apprentice pair and its effect on the creative outcome.

The approach consists of two parts: a master, which is a genetic algorithm, and an apprentice, which is an LSTM sequence-to-sequence model. While the master is in charge of the internal appreciation of the overall system as implemented in its fitness function, the apprentice plays a crucial role in the creative autonomy as it can learn its standards partially from its master and partially from its peers.

This paper focuses on the exploration of the master-apprentice approach from a social psychological point of view. By modelling the socialization of the apprentice into a creative society consisting of the master and peers, we seek to gain a deeper understanding of the phenomenon in terms of the overall creativity of the system. In addition, modelling the social aspects of a computationally creative system can help in understanding creativity as a social phenomenon in a broader sense (Saunders and Bown 2015).

We motivate the model of socialization based on research conducted on the field of social psychology, namely developmental psychology. We select the categorization of parenting styles presented by (Baumrind 1991) as the theoretical foundation of our work.

The creative task we are tackling in this paper is the creation of humorous movie titles delivering a food-related pun. This consists of taking an existing movie title such as *Beauty and the Beast* and making a pun out of it such as *Beauty and the Beets*. As people have been writing funny movie titles of this sort in a great abundance on the social media, we can gather parallel data easily.

Related Work

While pun generation has been vastly studied in the field of computational creativity (Ritchie 2005; Yu, Tan, and Wan 2018; He, Peng, and Liang 2019), we see that the most important contribution of our paper lies in the realm of social creativity. Therefore, we dedicate this section in describing some of the practical research conducted in the computational social creativity.

Research on an agent community consisting of self-organizing maps (Honkela and Winter 2003), although outside of the computational creativity paradigm, presents a way of simulating the emergence of language. The agents are capable of meaning negotiation and converging into a common language to communicate about edibility of different food items in their shared world.

Multi-agent systems have been studied in the context of novelty seeking in creative artifact generation (Linkola, Takala, and Toivonen 2016). In their study, the agents exert self-criticism and they can vote and veto on creative artifacts. Their findings suggest that multiple creative agents can reach to a higher number of novelty in their output than a single agent system.

A recent study (Hantula and Linkola 2018) has been conducted in social creativity in agent societies where the individuals are goal-aware. The individuals create artifacts of their own and peer up to collaborate with another agent. The agents are capable of learning a peer model that guides them in selecting a collaboration partner.

The papers discussed in this section, as well as other similar previously conducted work (Gabora 1995; Corneli and Jordanous 2015; Pagnutti, Compton, and Whitehead 2016), study mostly the collaboration of agents that have an equal social status, in contrast to our case where the social status is hierarchical. Therefore we find that there's need for conducting the study presented in this paper to shed some light into asymmetrical social relations in computational creativity.

Social Development

The master-apprentice approach gives us an intriguing test bed for modelling different social interactions between the master and the apprentice. With such a complex phenomenon as human social behavior, we are bound to limit our focus on a subarea of the phenomenon. In this section, we describe different psychological approaches in understanding socialization.

Socialization, i.e. becoming a part of a social group, is an important part of the psychological development of an individual. Even to such a degree that a child who is never exposed to other people will not develop a language nor an understanding of self. Socialization, thus seems to play a crucial role in higher-level cognitive development of everything that we consider to separate a man from an animal. Perhaps this great level of importance has been the reason a great many researchers have dedicated effort in unraveling this mystery.

The ecological systems theory of social development (Bronfenbrenner 1979) highlights the importance of bidirectionality of different social groups. An individual child is in the middle of the model, but just as the immediate close family affects on the child, the child is also an actor in the process of socialization. The theory identifies multiple different systems from close family all the way to the level of the society that play a role in the social development of a child. This theory is quite complex to model computationally.

A take, simpler to model, on the social development is that of parenting styles (Baumrind 1991). We find these findings more suitable as a starting point for modelling the socialization of the apprentice in our master-apprentice approach. The parenting styles can be divided into four main categories: authoritative, authoritarian, permissive and rejecting-neglecting. These categories deviate from each other on the two-fold axis of demandingness and responsiveness as seen in Figure 1.

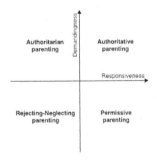

Figure 1: Parenting styles

The authoritative parents are high on both demandingness and responsiveness. They set rules, but the rules are negotiable. The parenting is more supportive than punitive in nature. The authoritarian parents, on the other hand, are low on responsiveness and high on demandingness. They set non-negotiable rules and expect obedience without explanation.

The permissive parents are low on demandingess and high on responsiveness. They are very lenient and avoid confrontation. The rejecting-neglecting parents, however, are low on both axis. They hardly engage in parenting, they offer little support and do not set any rules.

Creativity

The original research on the master-apprentice approach (Alnajjar and Hämäläinen 2018) used the creative tripod (Colton 2008) to define creativity in general and in the context of their work on creating movie titles satirical towards Saudi-Arabia by following the notions of the SPECS approach (Jordanous 2012). We use the same creative tripod framework to adapt their definition into our similar task of creating movie titles with food puns. This definition provides us with a reasoned way of conducting evaluation of the overall creativity of our systems.

The creative tripod requires three key notions to be present in a system in order for it to achieve creativity. These are *skill*, *imagination* and *appreciation*. All of these components must be present simultaneously in a creative system, or the system will lack creativity.

For our systems to exhibit skill, they will need to take a movie title as input and produce a new one with a food pun. As in the case of the earlier master-apprentice approach, the new humorous title should still communicate the original title, i.e. the original name of the movie should be recognizable.

Requirements for a pun are that it reassembles the original word in pronunciation and that it is humorous. According to (Oring 2003), *incongruity* results in humour if it is delivered in a playful fashion and accompanied by its resolution. Another, maybe a bit more concrete way of looking at humour, is seeing incongruity as a *surprise* and resolution as *coherence* c.f. (Brownell et al. 1983).

Surprise in the context of humor means that the brain forms an expectation and this expectation is then broken by the humorous element of the pun. Such is the case in the pun *Harry Potter and the Deathly Marshmallows* where the surprise is caused by the fact that the expected word *Hallows* is replaced by *Marshmallows*. For the pun to be coherent, it should make sense in the context of the original movie. In this case, a thought of deathly marshmallows attacking the Hogwarts, although bizarre, can still be seen as coherent.

For achieving appreciation, the systems will need to be able to assess the humorousness of the created pun in terms of surprise, coherence and sound similarity. In addition to the humour, the system should be able to evaluate the recognizability of the original title.

We define imagination by using the dichotomy of creativity introduced by (Boden 2004). This way of understanding creativity divides it in two different types: P-creativity and H-creativity. P-creativity is the minimal requirement we set for imagination of the systems, and it means that a creative entity should be able to come up with something that is novel to itself. H-creativity, on the other hand, refers to an innovation that is novel in a more global scale, i.e. nobody else has come up with a similar creative artifact before. While P-creativity is the minimum requirement, we consider H-creativity as a more desired requirement for imagination.

The Data

As our approach is to generate food related puns, we need a vocabulary consisting of food related terms. For this purpose we use the Historical Thesaurus of the Oxford English Dictionary[1]. We use all the nouns recorded under the topic *food and drink* in the *external world* taxonomy. This list contains 15,314 different nouns.

We extract real movie titles from the IMDB[2] (Internet movie database). As we want our movie title corpus to consist only of well known movies, we want to filter out all the less known indie movies. To achieve this, we filter out movies that have received less than 100,000 votes, leaving us with 1,661 movie titles. For the master and apprentices this is further limited to 1276 titles by filtering out the titles that consisted only of one word.

For parallel humorous movie title data (later peer data), we crawl comments on an Instagram post for an entertainment account[3]. People were encouraged to come up with creative movie titles containing a pun related to food. The total number of comments crawled is 16,088[4]. Then, we follow the same approach applied in (Alnajjar and Hämäläinen 2018) to map the crawled data to movie titles. In summary, we preprocess the text to remove any hashtags and mentions, and then we measure the character and word edit distances between the comments and movie titles. Finally, a comment is considered to be a punny variation of the matched movie title with the least edit distance, only if it had at most three word differences while ensuring that there exist at least one word matching the movie title. This process yields 9,294 human-authored movie titles containing a pun.

The Master-Apprentice Model

The master-apprentice model consists of a computationally creative genetic algorithm that implements the criteria set for appreciation in its fitness function and an apprentice that is an NMT (neural machine translation) model. The master generates parallel data for the apprentice to learn from, while the apprentice can also learn from its peers. In our setting, we have four different apprentices; one for each parenting style.

Master

Inspired by the work on slogan generation presented by Alnajjar, Hadaytullah, and Toivonen (2018), we employ a similar generator to act as a master in our model. In our case, the generator, which is a genetic algorithm, receives an original movie title as input and outputs an entire population of movie titles carrying a pun, based on the input movie title. The master makes use of the food related vocabulary described earlier to replace words in the original title while

optimizing multiple parameters to increase the aptness of the substitution and the punniness of the title. The following subsections elucidate the algorithm.

Evolutionary algorithm The first step in the evolutionary algorithm is producing the initial population, which will go through the process of evolution during a certain number of generations. The evolutionary algorithm employed is a standard $(\mu + \lambda)$[5] where mutation and crossover are applied to the current population to produce λ offspring. Individuals in the current population and their offspring are then evaluated by the algorithm to find the fittest μ number of individuals to survive to the next generation. Once the specified number of generations (10, in our case) is reached, the evolutionary process ends and returns the final population.

Initial Population The initial population consists of μ copies of the input movie title. For each copy, a randomly selected noun, adjective or verb is replaced with a random word from the vocabulary. We used *Spacy* (Honnibal and Montani 2017) to parse titles. We inflect the substituting words using *Pattern* (De Smedt and Daelemans 2012) to match the morphology of the original word when needed. The altered titles assemble the initial population.

Mutation and Crossover In our evolutionary algorithm, we implement one kind of mutation and crossover. The mutation process substitutes words in the individual in the same fashion as done in the creation of the initial population. The crossover employed is a standard single-point crossover, i.e. a random point in individuals is selected and words to the right of the point are switched between them.

Evaluation In our evaluation metric, we propose four internal evaluation dimensions to measure the fitness of an individual. These dimensions are (1) prosody, (2) semantic similarity to "food", (3) semantic similarity to the original word, and (4) number of altered words. The first two dimensions are maximized, whereas the last two are minimized.

The prosody dimension is a weighted sum of four prosody sub-features, which are consonance, assonance, rhyme and alliteration. This dimension measures the sound similarity between the original word and its substitution. To measure the sound similarity, we use *espeak-ng tool*[6] to generate IPA (international phonetic alphabet) transcriptions for assessing the prosody.

To measure the semantic similarity between two words, we employ a pre-trained *Glove* model[7] with 6 billion tokens and a dimension size of 300. The model is trained on Wikipedia and English Gigaword Fifth Edition corpus. Using the semantic model, the next dimension computes the maximum semantic similarity of words in the title to the word "food".

The third dimension measures the mean of the semantic similarity of new words to their original corresponding word. We minimize this dimension to increase surprise, with

---

[1]http://www.oed.com/thesaurus

[2]Dumps from https://datasets.imdbws.com/

[3]https://www.instagram.com/p/BsWki-PFbMO/

[4]Crawled on the second of February

[5]We set both to 100 empirically.

[6]https://github.com/espeak-ng/espeak-ng

[7]https://nlp.stanford.edu/projects/glove/

the idea that a lower semantic similarity between the original word and its substitute would result in a bigger surprise.

The last dimension keeps track of the number of words modified in comparison to the original title. Minimizing this dimension motivates that less substitutions are made to the title, which makes it more recognizable.

These are the criteria based on which the fitness of individuals is evaluated at the end of each generation to let only the best ones survive to the next generation.

Selection and Filtering To reduce having a dominating dimension and motivate generating titles with diverse and balanced scores on all four dimensions, we opt for a non-dominant sorting algorithm –*NSGA-II*– (Deb et al. 2002) as the selection algorithm.

During each iteration of the evolution, the current population and its offspring go through a filtering phase which filters out any duplicate titles.

Final Verdict On top of individual evaluation metrics, we introduce master's final verdict, which is a way of telling whether the master likes the generated title. The final verdict of the master is a binary decision, i.e. an individual is either good or not. In practice, the final verdict is defined as conditional thresholds on each dimension. These thresholds are 1) a positive non-zero value for prosody, 2) a positive non-zero semantic similarity to "food", 3) a semantic similarity less than 0.5 of the new word to its original and 4) not more than 50 percent change of content words.

The master uses this functionality to express its liking to titles outside of its own creations such as those created by the apprentice. Whenever we talk about the master liking something in this paper, we mean that the final verdict has a Boolean value of true.

Apprentice

For the apprentices we use OpenNMT (Klein et al. 2017), which implements an RNN based sequence to sequence model. The model has two RNN encoding layers and two RNN decoding layers.

The attention mechanism is the general global attention formulated by (Luong, Pham, and Manning 2015). The difference to the OpenNMT default parameters in our system is that we use the copy attention mechanism which makes it possible for the model to copy words from the source. This is useful since the task is to translate within the same language.

All of the apprentice models described in this paper have been trained by using the same random seed to make their intercomparison possible.

Different Parenting Styles

We model computationally the four different parenting styles, authoritarian, authoritative, permissive and rejecting-neglecting, in the way the master interacts with the apprentice during the training process of the NMT model.

The training process is done iteratively. In each iteration, the apprentice is trained for 1000 training steps. After each iteration, the apprentice produces an output based on the 1276 popular IMDB movie titles. This output is then evaluated by the master accordingly to the parenting style in question and adjustments are made to the training data based on the master's parenting. The apprentices are trained for 20 iterations.

The Authoritarian Master only lets the apprentice learn from its own output. The apprentice is not exposed to any of the peer data and the apprentice's own creations are not taken into account.

The Authoritative Master lets the apprentice learn from its own creations and those peers who it considers good enough by the final verdict (this means 2446 titles). The apprentice can show its creations to the master after each training iteration, out of which the master picks the ones it likes and adds them to the training material of the apprentice. The training of the NMT model continues with the modified corpus.

The Permissive Master lets the apprentice learn from its own creations and all of the peer data. When the apprentice presents its own creations at the end of a training iteration, the master praises them all and adds them to the training data.

The Rejecting-Neglecting Master does not care about the apprentice. The apprentice has no choice but to learn from its peers. The apprentice does not learn from its own creations because it receives no support from the master.

Training the Apprentice

The master is run once to create its own movie titles with food related puns. This parallel data of 8306 titles is shared across the different parenting styles. During the training process of the apprentice, the master does not generate new titles of its own, but only interferes in the selection of the parallel data used in the next training iteration as described in the sections above.

After each iteration, we calculate BLEU score (Papineni et al. 2002) and a uni-gram PINC score (Chen and Dolan 2011) for the outputs of the apprentices. We compare the outputs both to the training material coming from the master and the material from the peers. For each title generated by the apprentice, we take the maximum BLEU and minimum PINC score and take an average of them for each iteration.

BLEU score is traditionally used in machine translation to evaluate how good the final translation is in terms of a gold standard. We, however, do not use BLEU as a final evaluation metric, but rather use it to shed some light into how closely the outputs of the apprentices resemble those of the master or the peer written titles. BLEU measures the similarity, whereas PINC measures divergence from the original data. In other words, the higher the BLEU, the more closely the apprentice imitates and the higher the PINC the less it imitates the master or the peers.

As indicated by Figure 2, the authoritarian scenario, where the training data consists only of the master's output, starts quickly producing the output most similar to the master. Where as the authoritative scenario leads to a bit less similarity to the master. The effect of the peer data is

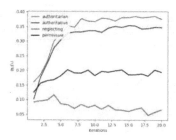

Figure 2: BLEU when comparing to the master

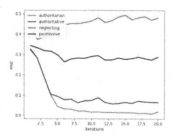

Figure 3: PINC when comparing to the master

very well visible in the permissive and neglecting scenarios. The PINC scores in Figure 3 show the other side of the coin where the authoritative and authoritarian scenarios are the least divergent and the permissive and neglecting ones the most divergent.

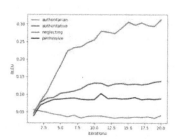

Figure 4: BLEU when comparing to peers

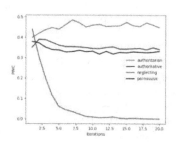

Figure 5: PINC when comparing to peers

When we do the BLEU comparison to the peer data as seen in Figure 4, we can see that only the neglecting scenario leads to high similarity with the peers, where as the other scenarios are still quite low, the lowest being the authoritarian scenario. The PINC scores tell a similar story in Figure 5, where the neglecting scenario leads to the least amount of divergence, leaving the authoritarian scenario the most divergent.

Results and Evaluation

In this section, we show some of the results produced by the different systems. In addition, we evaluate the different parenting style scenarios after each iteration with the master's appreciation function. Later, an evaluation is conducted by humans.

Results and Master's Liking

Results from the approaches can be seen in Table 1. The master did not produce any training data for the last two titles in the examples. Looking at these results qualitatively, in broad lines, the permissive and neglecting scenarios produced worse output than the ones exposed to the master's training data. The apprentice exposed to authoritarian parenting struggles in producing output for titles not present in the training data. The authoritative scenario leads to the most consistent results. The quantitative human evaluation in the next section is used to verify these initial observations.

Another way to look at the results is to use the appreciation metrics implemented in the master. Figure 6 shows the percentage of how many titles the master liked after each training iteration.

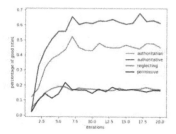

Figure 6: Master's liking of the output

As we can see, the appreciation the master has ranks the authoritarian and authoritative scenarios higher than the permissive and neglecting ones. Even in the authoritarian case, the master does not like all of the output produced by the apprentice, which shows that the appreciation learned by the apprentices is different from the one implemented in the master.

It is interesting to see to what extent the master's liking correlates with the evaluation results of the human judges. This can reveal more information about the adequacy of the appreciation of the master in this creative task. Or does the master's appreciation only tell about obedience when applied to the apprentices' output?

original	master	authoritarian	authoritative	permissive	neglecting
the butterfly effect	*the brewery effect*	*the butterfly kimchi*	*the butterfly chicken*	*the butterfly effect*	*the lasagna effect lazarus*
how to train your dragon	*how to train your pepperoni*	*how to train your avocado*	*how to train your pepperoni*	*how to train your bacon*	*how to train your bacon*
fantastic beasts and where to find them	—	*fantastic ordinary and where to find*	*fantastic beets and where to find them*	*fantastic beefs and where to find them*	*fantastic beets and where to find them*
under the skin	—	*under the cereals*	*under the silver cake*	*under the 13th*	*fryday the 13*

Table 1: Examples of the final output of the different models

Evaluation Questions

In this section we provide some reasoning in our selection of the evaluation questions that are presented to the human judges. Earlier, we defined the creativity in the case of pun generation using the creative tripod as our theoretical framework. This means that on a higher level, our evaluation questions should evaluate *skill*, *appreciation* and *imagination*.

Skill Our definition for skill stated that the system should be able to take an existing movie title and produce a food related pun as an output. A further requirement was that the original title should be recognizable from the generated one.

1. The title has a pun in it
2. The title is related to food
3. The original title is recognizable

The evaluation questions described above are designed to evaluate the requirements set for skill. We evaluate whether a pun is perceived and whether the new title relates to food separately, as it might be that the replacement word delivers a pun, but is not food related or vice-versa.

Appreciation We defined appreciation from the humor stand point. A good title with a pun is also funny. For something to be funny, i.e. humorous, the pun has to exhibit coherence and surprise.

4. The title is humorous
5. The pun is surprising
6. The pun makes sense in the context of the original movie

We choose to evaluate the overall humor value of the title separately from the components that constitute it. The last two questions are designed to evaluate surprise and coherence respectively.

Imagination We used Boden's dichotomy to establish the definition of imagination. The minimal requirement was set to P-creativity. However, P-creativity can easily be verified by looking at the training data and the final output, if the output is different from the training material, there is P-creativity. Therefore, we use human judges to assess the H-creativity of the outputs.

7. The pun in the title is obvious
8. The pun in the title sounds familiar

If the pun is obvious, it probably is not too H-creative, as an obvious pun could be said by just about anyone, also if the pun sounds familiar, it has probably been said by someone before.

Human Evaluation

We take a random sample of 20 original movie titles that were only present in the training data provided by the master, 20 titles that were only present in the peer data and 20 titles that were in both sources of parallel data. We evaluate the creative output of each apprentice for these randomly sampled titles. In addition, we evaluate the master's output for the 40 titles of the sample it had generated movie title puns for. As the master has generated multiple creative titles per original title, we pick one randomly for each original title. Altogether, we are evaluating 280 computer created titles.

The evaluation was conducted on a crowd-sourcing platform called Figure Eight[8]. The platform assigned people to conduct evaluation in such a way that each title was evaluated by 35 different users. The users could choose how many titles they wanted to evaluate. The results of the evaluation are show in Table 2. In the Training column, *both*, *peer only* and *master only* indicate whether the original title was only present in the master produced training data, peer produced training data or in both respectively.

The authoritarian scenario didn't get the best average score for any of the test questions and neither did the master. They both score particularly low on the Q2, which reflects the fact that some of the words in the HTOED food and drink taxonomy were only loosely related to food such as *steam* and *spit*. It is interesting to note that the authoritarian scenario gets the best results for Q3, Q6 and Q7 for titles it did not encounter in the training data, in other words it has developed an appreciation of its own that does not just mimic what the master produces and fail otherwise. In light of these results, we can deduce that the master produced worse titles with food puns than real people, which left both the master and the authoritarian scenario without the first place on any of the test questions.

The authoritative scenario, which was the highest ranking one according to master's liking as seen in Figure 6, got the best results for Q1 and Q5. This means that it succeeds the best in the main task of generating puns and they end up being the most surprising ones. It is also the only one that produces consistently good results (above 3 on the average) for all training test sets for Q1-Q6, unfortunately the results for Q7 and Q8 are also above 3 on the average meaning that it does not rank high on H-creativity.

The same consistency can not be perceived in the the per-

---
[8]https://www.figure-eight.com/

Style	Training	Q1		Q2		Q3		Q4		Q5		Q6		Q7		Q8	
		μ_x	SD	μ_x	SD	μ_x	SD	μ_x	SD	μ_x	SD	μ_x	SD	μ_x	SD	μ_x	SD
authoritarian	both	**3.35**	1.08	2.65	1.26	3.33	1.06	**3.02**	1.10	**3.08**	0.99	3.03	1.01	3.16	0.99	3.10	1.03
authoritarian	peer only	2.97	1.18	2.14	1.17	**3.44**	1.13	2.66	1.15	2.82	1.08	**3.10**	1.11	**3.03**	1.12	3.11	1.13
authoritarian	master only	3.34	1.07	**2.89**	1.28	3.30	1.05	3.00	1.12	3.07	1.05	3.04	1.02	3.12	1.02	**3.07**	1.04
authoritative	both	3.43	1.08	3.09	1.31	3.28	1.12	3.08	1.16	3.08	1.05	3.02	1.05	**3.22**	1.06	**3.13**	1.05
authoritative	peer only	3.41	1.14	**3.23**	1.35	3.37	1.21	3.13	1.16	3.07	1.08	3.08	1.09	3.24	1.10	3.16	1.13
authoritative	master only	*3.47*	1.03	3.15	1.33	**3.41**	1.08	**3.17**	1.11	*3.16*	1.02	3.16	1.04	3.28	1.01	3.24	1.06
master	both	3.38	1.07	**2.79**	1.28	3.29	1.06	3.07	1.12	**3.09**	1.04	**3.10**	1.06	3.22	1.02	3.14	1.05
master	master only	**3.40**	1.07	2.61	1.30	**3.34**	1.11	**3.10**	1.15	3.09	1.02	3.04	1.03	**3.17**	1.04	**3.11**	1.06
neglecting	both	**3.45**	1.11	*3.28*	1.32	**3.34**	1.11	*3.28*	1.12	*3.16*	1.06	3.12	1.04	3.21	1.08	3.22	1.07
neglecting	peer only	3.36	1.07	3.02	1.37	3.31	1.11	3.12	1.15	3.09	1.02	**3.14**	1.04	3.19	1.02	**3.14**	1.06
neglecting	master only	3.28	1.13	2.87	1.35	3.34	1.12	3.09	1.14	3.05	1.05	3.07	1.06	**3.15**	1.06	3.18	1.08
permissive	both	3.23	1.18	2.67	1.38	3.59	1.06	**3.06**	1.13	**3.08**	1.08	*3.30*	1.04	3.21	1.07	3.30	1.10
permissive	peer only	3.05	1.19	**2.87**	1.39	3.25	1.18	2.88	1.13	2.88	1.09	3.00	1.08	2.99	1.11	3.04	1.14
permissive	master only	3.09	1.23	2.32	1.24	*3.64*	1.11	2.88	1.15	2.91	1.12	3.07	1.15	*2.98*	1.13	*3.04*	1.12

Table 2: Mean and standard deviation.

Style	Q1	Q2	Q3	Q4	Q5	Q6	Q7	Q8
authoritarian	78.33%	31.67%	83.33%	31.67%	48.33%	68.33%	70.00%	68.33%
authoritative	**93.33%**	**60.00%**	83.33%	56.67%	63.33%	66.67%	90.00%	70.00%
master	92.50%	37.50%	**87.50%**	62.50%	60.00%	65.00%	80.00%	**67.50%**
neglecting	86.67%	**60.00%**	81.67%	**66.67%**	**65.00%**	**73.33%**	75.00%	78.33%
permissive	66.67%	33.33%	85.00%	43.33%	46.67%	**73.33%**	**68.33%**	71.67%

Table 3: Percentage of movie titles having an average score by judges greater than 3

missive case as scores below 3 are common across the test questions. It however, manages to score the best for Q3 and Q7-Q8, in other words, it can achieve the best H-creativity and the original titles can be the most recognizable, although not consistently so. This shows, that even though the appreciation the master has might not be spot on, as it is not able to produce the best scoring titles, having moderation on the peer data and critical assessment of the apprentice generated results during the training by the master, has a positive effect on the consistency of the results. In the permissive scenario, the apprentice was exposed to everything without criticism and in the authoritative some criticism was used to filer the training data, which made the authoritative scenario more consistent, but less H-creative.

Finally, the neglecting scenario gets the best scores for the Q2, Q4 and Q5. It is the best one at producing humorous, surprising and food related titles. It is quite consistent with only the results for Q2 with previously unseen titles giving a score that is inferior to 3. The good results of the neglecting scenario serve as an additional proof to the fact that the output of the master is worse than human written titles.

Table 3 shows the results form another stand point. The table shows overall how many titles got the average rating above 3 for each test question. These numbers are in line with what was previously discussed about the Table 2. The authoritarian scenario leads to the worst performance, but this time master gets the highest percentage point of titles above 3 for Q3. In the authoritative scenario most of the titles have a clear pun and are related to food with the highest percentage point. The permissive scenario holds the best percentage points for Q6 and Q7. And the neglecting gets the best percentage points in Q2, Q4, Q5 and Q6.

Discussion and Future Work

The evaluation results were not completely in line with what we can observe by looking at the titles output by the different methods by ourselves. This raises the question whether our definition for creativity in movie title puns is adequate and whether the evaluation questions we formulated based on the definition really measure what they were designed to measure. Because we have worked with a clear definition for creativity in this paper, it is possible to take this under a critical study in the future. We also find evident that qualitative research on the output titles with respect to the quantitative results we got from the human judges is needed to evaluate the evaluation itself.

Having a master with appreciation filter the parallel data of the apprentice was beneficial for consistency (see authoritative vs permissive). Although the evaluation results showed that the appreciation is not in par with that of a real human, the implication remains that a good external appreciation can be beneficial for the learning outcome of the apprentice model. As we used a rather generic NMT model for the apprentice, our findings might be of a use in more traditional context of sequence-to-sequence models such as machine translation, text summarization or paraphrasing.

For now, the master and apprentice have been studied in a social vacuum, where peer data is the only link to the surrounding world. However, in the future it would be fruitful to see how the creative outcome changes when the master and the apprentice are exposed to a more complex social system such as the one described by Bronfenbrenner (Bronfenbrenner 1979). In such a society, the master would also be under a social pressure in changing its own standards of appreciation.

Conclusions

This work has presented one of the first contributions to the field of computational social creativity where the computationally creative agents are in a hierarchical social relation. This asymmetry offers an intriguing setting for studying socialization of computational agents from the creativity perspective.

Despite building our definition of creativity upon an existing theory and formulating the test questions based on the definition, the quantitative evaluation left many questions unanswered. The results presented in this paper call for qualitative evaluation to understand the phenomenon of evaluation in this particular context.

Nevertheless, our findings suggest that having appreciation in parenting, or training, an NMT model can be of a benefit. The applicability of these finding into sequence-to-sequence deep learning models in a more generalized fashion is an interesting research question on its own right.

References

Alnajjar, K., and Hämäläinen, M. 2018. A Master-Apprentice Approach to Automatic Creation of Culturally Satirical Movie Titles. In *Proceedings of the 11th International Conference on Natural Language Generation (INLG)*, 274—283.

Alnajjar, K.; Hadaytullah, H.; and Toivonen, H. 2018. "Talent, Skill and Support." A method for automatic creation of slogans. In *Proceedings of the Ninth International Conference on Computational Creativity*, 88–95.

Baumrind, D. 1991. Parenting styles and adolescent development. *The Encyclopedia of Adolescence* 758–772.

Boden, M. A. 2004. *The creative mind: Myths and mechanisms*. Routledge.

Bronfenbrenner, U. 1979. *The ecology of human development*. Harvard university press.

Brownell, H. H.; Michel, D.; Powelson, J.; and Gardner, H. 1983. Surprise but not coherence: Sensitivity to verbal humor in right-hemisphere patients. *Brain and Language* 18(1):20 – 27.

Chen, D. L., and Dolan, W. B. 2011. Collecting highly parallel data for paraphrase evaluation. In *Proceedings of the 49th Annual Meeting of the Association for Computational Linguistics: Human Language Technologies-Volume 1*, 190–200.

Colton, S. 2008. Creativity Versus the Perception of Creativity in Computational Systems. In *AAAI Spring Symposium: Creative Intelligent Systems*, Technical Report SS-08-03, 14—20.

Corneli, J., and Jordanous, A. 2015. Implementing feedback in creative systems: a workshop approach. In *Proceedings of the First International Conference on AI and Feedback-Volume 1407*, 10–17. CEUR-WS. org.

De Smedt, T., and Daelemans, W. 2012. Pattern for Python. *Journal of Machine Learning Research* 13:2063–2067.

Deb, K.; Pratap, A.; Agarwal, S.; and Meyarivan, T. 2002. A fast and elitist multiobjective genetic algorithm: Nsga-ii.

IEEE Transactions on Evolutionary Computation 6(2):182–197.

Gabora, L. 1995. Meme and variations: A computer model of cultural evolution. *1993 Lectures in Complex Systems* 471–486.

Hantula, O., and Linkola, S. 2018. Towards goal-aware collaboration in artistic agent societies. In *Proceedings of the Ninth International Conference on Computational Creativity*.

He, H.; Peng, N.; and Liang, P. 2019. Pun generation with surprise. *arXiv preprint arXiv:1904.06828*.

Honkela, T., and Winter, J. 2003. *Simulating language learning in community of agents using self-organizing maps*. Helsinki University of Technology.

Honnibal, M., and Montani, I. 2017. spaCy 2: Natural Language Understanding with Bloom Embeddings, Convolutional Neural Networks and Incremental Parsing. *To appear*.

Jordanous, A. 2012. A standardised procedure for evaluating creative systems: Computational creativity evaluation based on what it is to be creative. *Cognitive Computation* 4(3):246–279.

Klein, G.; Kim, Y.; Deng, Y.; Senellart, J.; and Rush, A. M. 2017. OpenNMT: Open-Source Toolkit for Neural Machine Translation. In *Proc. ACL*.

Linkola, S.; Takala, T.; and Toivonen, H. 2016. Novelty-seeking multi-agent systems. In *Proceedings of The Seventh International Conference on Computational Creativity*.

Luong, M.-T.; Pham, H.; and Manning, C. D. 2015. Effective approaches to attention-based neural machine translation. *arXiv preprint arXiv:1508.04025*.

Oring, E. 2003. Engaging humor. *Urbana and Chicago: University of Illinois Press*.

Pagnutti, J.; Compton, K.; and Whitehead, J. 2016. Do you like this art i made you: introducing techne, a creative artbot commune. In *Proceedings of 1st International Joint Conference of DiGRA and FDG*.

Papineni, K.; Roukos, S.; Ward, T.; and Zhu, W.-J. 2002. Bleu: a method for automatic evaluation of machine translation. In *Proceedings of the 40th annual meeting on association for computational linguistics*, 311–318.

Ritchie, G. 2005. Computational mechanisms for pun generation. In *Proceedings of the Tenth European Workshop on Natural Language Generation (ENLG-05)*.

Saunders, R., and Bown, O. 2015. Computational social creativity. *Artificial life* 21(3):366–378.

Yu, Z.; Tan, J.; and Wan, X. 2018. A neural approach to pun generation. In *Proceedings of the 56th Annual Meeting of the Association for Computational Linguistics (Volume 1: Long Papers)*, volume 1, 1650–1660.

Let's FACE it. Finnish Poetry Generation with Aesthetics and Framing

Mika Hämäläinen
Department of Digital Humanities
University of Helsinki
mika.hamalainen@helsinki.fi

Khalid Alnajjar
Department of Computer Science (HIIT)
University of Helsinki
khalid.alnajjar@helsinki.fi

Abstract

We present a creative poem generator for the morphologically rich Finnish language. Our method falls into the master-apprentice paradigm, where a computationally creative genetic algorithm teaches a BRNN model to generate poetry. We model several parts of poetic aesthetics in the fitness function of the genetic algorithm, such as sonic features, semantic coherence, imagery and metaphor. Furthermore, we justify the creativity of our method based on the FACE theory on computational creativity and take additional care in evaluating our system by automatic metrics for concepts together with human evaluation for aesthetics, framing and expressions.

1 Introduction

This paper explores the topic of computational creativity in the case of poem generation in Finnish. Our work does not only aim to generate, but rather create poems automatically. We take the FACE model (Colton et al., 2011) for computational creativity as our definition of creativity. Through this model, we motivate and evaluate creativity exhibited by our system.

Methodologically, our work embraces the master-apprentice method (Alnajjar and Hämäläinen, 2018) used in the past for computationally creative tasks. This means using a creative genetic algorithm as a master to teach an apprentice which is sequence-to-sequence neural network model. This way the overall system can approximate creative autonomy (Jennings, 2010) if the apprentice was to be exposed to data originating from another source than the master. For further discussion on the topic of autonomy, see the original work establishing the master-apprentice method.

We pay special attention to evaluation of our system, and we motivate it through the FACE model. A creative system should be evaluated in terms of what has actually been modelled rather than on an ad-hoc and unjustified fashion. Additionally, our contribution lies on the fact that the aesthetics of our system are motivated by existing non-computational literature in poetry analysis. Furthermore, our system is capable of adjusting its aesthetics based on existing poetry.

Our work sheds some more light into the nature of a master-apprentice system. Especially by seeking to answer the question of multiple masters raised in the original work on the topic (Alnajjar and Hämäläinen, 2018), which the authors left unanswered.

2 Related Work

While poetry generation has been tackled a number of times before by multiple authors (Gervás, 2001; Toivanen et al., 2012; Misztal and Indurkhya, 2014; Oliveira et al., 2017), and an excellent overview is provided by Oliveira (2017) on the recent state of the research, we dedicate this section in describing the most recent work conducted in the field after the aforementioned overview paper.

TwitSong (Lamb and Brown, 2019) mines a corpus for verses to be used in poetry based on how well they rhyme together. They score the verses in poems by four metrics (*meter, emotion, topicality* and *imagery)* and use a genetic algorithm to edit the worst scoring verse in the poem. However, they only assess poems on a verse level and their algorithm lacks poem level metrics (i.e. each verse is considered individually and not as a part of a whole). They base their evaluation on comparing generated poetry of different groups based on how the genetic algorithm was used. They use very broad questions such as *which poem is more creative* or *which poem has better imagery*. This

290

is potentially problematic as broad questions open more room for subjective interpretation.

Last year, a myriad of work on generation of Chinese poetry with machine learning methods was conducted. Research ranging from mutual reinforcement learning (Yi et al., 2018) and conditional variational autoencoders (Li et al., 2018) to sequence-to-sequence Bi-LSTMs (Yang et al., 2018) was presented. However, none of these methods has been motivated from the point of view of computational creativity, but rather serve for a purely generative purpose.

The work conducted by Colton et al. (2012), although not recent, deserves special attention, as they had used the same FACE model as a basis in their poem generation. They take a template based approach to generating poems from current news articles. Unfortunately they do not provide an evaluation of the generated poetry, which makes meaningful comparison difficult.

The work presented by us in this paper has to deal with the rich morphosyntax of Finnish, which is an NLG problem far from solved. Hämäläinen (2018) presents a solution for this problem in their Finnish poem generator. However, their generator relies on predefined rule-based structures, whereas our aim is to have a system with more structural versatility, and yet the capability of coping with the morphosyntax.

3 Creativity

In order to separate our system from generative non-creative systems, we have to provide some justification as to why our system would exhibit creativity in the first place. For this reason, we follow the SPECS approach (Jordanous, 2012) that has been designed to evaluate creativity in a reasoned fashion. The approach requires creativity to be defined first on an abstract level, and then, following the abstract definition, creativity should be defined in the context of the creative task that is to be solved. After establishing these definitions, creativity of the system should then be evaluated based on the definitions.

3.1 Creativity in General

For an abstract level definition of creativity, we use FACE (Colton et al., 2011). The theory divides creative act into two categories, one is the ground level generative act of producing an artefact and the other is on the level of the process. Both of these categories are represented in the four aspects of creativity: framing, aesthetics, concept and expression.

Framing consists of outputting a framing for a creative artefact, and the process that generates this output. The framing should be an explanation in natural language, for instance, putting the created artefact into a historical and cultural context or describing the processes of creating the output artefact. In other words, framing can be used as an additional persuasive or explanatory message that is delivered to the human perceiving the artefact produced by a computational system.

Aesthetics consist of a function measuring the aesthetic quality of the output and/or the program producing it. On the process level, FACE takes into account how the aesthetic measures came to be in the system. The system should be able to assess its own work and rate its creations. This aesthetic measure can also be used to computationally assess artefacts produced by other systems or humans.

Concept is used to refer to the program that generates creative artefacts on the ground level. And on the process level it refers to how such a program was generated. Finally, the ground level expression is the creative output, or artefact, generated by the system, whereas the process level of expression describes the method for generating output for a given input.

3.2 Creativity for Our Poem Generator

As framing can exists in many different forms according to the original FACE model, we follow a more narrowed down notion of framing, which is the intention of the computer in creating artefacts (Charnley et al., 2012). In other words, the computer should be able to output a justification explaining what certain aspects of the poem mean. The importance of framing has recently been highlighted in the literature (Cook et al., 2019).

Framing does not have to be a creative act on its own. In our case, the process of coming up with a framing is a template based approach that conveys the intent of the creative program in producing the output poem. This intent, on the other hand is captured by the aesthetic function of the creative system. Therefore, the framing produced should explain the poem in terms of the aesthetic measures.

Poetry as a genre showcases a wide diversity in

terms of aesthetics; ranging from epic poetry following a strict meter to modern free form poetry. Even to a degree that the poetic genre has become fragmented ever since the 20th century (Juntunen, 2012). This diversity is not just limited to the level of structure, but is also reflected in meaning - some forms of poetry are meant to be read and interpreted literally, where as others rely on indirect communication such as symbolism and metaphors (see Kantokorpi et al., 1990). In our work, we are not aiming to model the poetic genre as a whole, but rather define a set of aesthetic functions that capture different aspects in poetry ranging from the structural to the meaning.

In terms of structure, our system should be able to assess rhyming in its various forms (alliteration, assonance, consonance and full rhymes) and the meter of the poetry as defined by poetic foot and syllable count.

For meaning, our system should be able appreciate the presence of metaphors, the semantic coherence of the words forming the poem and in especial the presence of words forming different semantic fields and the semantic difference of these fields as an indicator of tension built by the choice of words in a poem (cf. Lotman, 1974).

Certain poems paint a mental image in the mind of the reader; this qualia[1] provoking aspect of poetry is called *imagery*. As it is extremely difficult for a computer to assess such rich mental sensory phenomena provoked by poetry in humans, we have to reduce the aesthetics related to imagery to a more computationally manageable level, namely that of sentiment. Sentiments expressed in a poem can be indicators of the potential mood evoked by the sensory imagery in the poem. Another indicator of imagery is the use of concrete expressions (see Burroway, 2007).

Although the list of aesthetic measures is predefined, from the point of view of the process, our system should be able learn to adjust its aesthetic measures based on existing poetry. Furthermore, we aim towards a system that can learn aesthetics of its own on its own level of abstraction, hence the use of apprentice.

In our case, the system consists of two concepts. One of them is a genetic algorithm (master) that has been defined by us, the programmers. The role of the master is to produce expressions through a search informed by the aesthetic functions. These expression are used to train the second concept, which is a sequence-to-sequence BRNN model (apprentice). This way, the overall system is given the capability of producing new concepts of its own.

The expressions output by the system are computationally created Finnish poems. Ultimately, we evaluate the expressions produced by the apprentice with real humans and by the master's aesthetic measures.

3.3 Data

We use the 6,189 Finnish poems that are available on Wikisources[2] as our poem corpus. We use the Finnish dependency parser (Haverinen et al., 2014) to parse the poems for morphological features, syntactic relations, part of speech and lemma for each word. The parsing is done on a verse-level. We split each poem into stanzas as divided in Wikisources. From now on we refer to a stanza of an existing poem simply as a poem. The reason for this is to have shorter poems to deal with in the generation step. This is especially important for the human evaluation as shorter poems can be evaluated more accurately, as longer poems have more room for unintentional characteristics that can be interpreted too positively by human judges, such as a perceivably deeper meaning that is due to the mere fact of having more context to read more into. After splitting the poems into stanzas, we have a total of 34,988 poems.

We use the word embeddings[3] that have been trained on the Finnish Internet Parsebank (Kanerva et al., 2014). We prefer this model for two reasons: first it has been trained on a 1.5 billion token corpus that is big on the Finnish scale and second it has been trained on lemmas, which is an important factor for a highly agglutinating language such as Finnish. In order to generate grammatical Finnish, the words need to be inflected. This step is easier if the replacement words are already in a lemmatized from.

4 Generating Poetry

The master-apprentice approach outlined in Alnajjar and Hämäläinen (2018) consists of a creative master, which is a genetic algorithm, and an apprentice, which is a sequence-to-sequence model.

---

[1]For more on the problem of qualia, see (Chalmers, 1995)

[2]https://fi.wikisource.org
[3]http://bionlp-www.utu.fi/fin-vector-space-models/fin-word2vec-lemma.bin

292

In this part of the paper, we describe how the aesthetics are implemented in the master and how it is used to generate poems for the apprentice to learn from.

In this paper, we experiment with two different masters, which will learn the weights for their aesthetic functions form poems of different eras. We use these masters to train one apprentice for each of them. In addition, we train one apprentice, which will learn from both of the masters.

4.1 Master

The master is a genetic algorithm following the implementation presented in Alnajjar et al. (2018). In practice, the algorithm takes in a random poem from the poem corpus and uses it to produce an initial population of 100 individuals. These individuals produce an offspring of another 100 individuals that go through mutation and crossover, and at the end of each generation the individuals are scored according to the aesthetic functions defined later in this section. The 100 fittest individuals are selected with NSGA-II algorithm (Deb et al., 2002) to survive to the next generation. This process is done for 50 generations.

All individuals in the initial population are based on a randomly selected poem and a randomly picked theme word. The theme is expanded into the 30 most semantically similar words to the theme word using word2vec (Mikolov et al., 2013). Each poem in the initial population is assigned a random theme out of the 30 semantically similar words to the theme. Additionally, we modify each poem in the initial population once by using the mutation function. This is applied to have more variety of poems in the initial population given that all of them are based on the same original poem from the corpus.

In mutation, a random content word is picked in the poem and it is replaced by a word related to the input theme (assigned to the poem) or by a word that is similar to the original one, while ensuring that the new replacement matches the original in terms of its part-of-speech. To obtain words that are related to the input theme, we build a semantic relatedness model following Xiao et al. (2016) using the flat 5-gram data provided by Kanerva et al. (2014) as the corpus. Regarding the semantic similarity to the original word, we utilize the word2vec word embeddings model. The space of candidate replacements consists of the top

1,000 and 300 (empirically chosen) semantically related and similar words, respectively. Out of these candidates, only words that match the part-of-speech of the original word, based on Uralic-NLP (Hämäläinen, 2019), are considered in the random selection.

In terms of the crossover, we employ a single-point crossover on a verse-level where one point in both individuals is selected at random and verses to the right of that point are swapped.

As mutations and crossovers are bound to break the morphosyntax of Finnish, the new words are always inflected to match the original morphology with UralicNLP and Omorfi (Pirinen et al., 2017). This will account for morphological agreement, but not for case government. In case government, the case of the complements of the verb depends on the verb itself. For this reason, we inflect words with an object relation with Syntax Maker (Hämäläinen and Rueter, 2018) to produce a grammatical surface form even if the predicate verb is changed.

4.1.1 Aesthetics

To assess the sonic structure of poetry the following rule-based aesthetic functions are defined on an inter-verse level: full rhyme, assonance and consonance. These count the number of rhyming words between verses of the poem. Alliteration is a metric calculated within a verse, as this type of rhyming occurs typically inside of a verse in Finnish poetry. As Finnish spelling is almost one to one mapping with phonology, we can do this on a character level without the need to approximate the pronunciation.

Meter is captured by two aesthetic functions: the number of syllables and the distribution of long and short syllables within a verse. These two functions are again solved by simple rules. The master rates higher the meter it has learned from its training corpus.

A previous attempt to capture imagery in the literature is by comparing the number of abstract and non-abstract words with the hypothesis that non-abstract words provoke more mental imagery (Kao and Jurafsky, 2012). However, this notion can be used only as a proxy to the quantity of imagery in poetry, but it tells nothing about the nature of the provoked imagery. For this reason, we have also decided to use sentiment as an indicator of the mood of the mental image painted by the poem.

For abstractness of words we use an existing

dataset for English that maps 40,000 common English words to an average concreteness score as annotated by humans on a 5-point Likert scale (Brysbaert et al., 2014). We translate this data in Finnish with a Wiktionary based online dictionary[4] in such a way that we consider the three topmost translations that are verbs, nouns or adjectives for each English word. To deal with polysemy, if multiple English words translate into one Finnish word, we take the average of the concreteness values of the English words for the Finnish word. If the concreteness value is greater or equal to 3, the word is considered concrete. The aesthetic function gives a ratio of concrete words over concrete and abstract words in the poem.

For sentiment, due to the lack of resources for Finnish, we use a recent state of the art method (Feng and Wan, 2019) that can learn sentiment prediction for English with annotated data and use the model for other languages by bilingual word embeddings. We train the model with sentiment annotated data for English from the OpeNER project (Agerri et al., 2013). We use their method to map the pretrained Finnish and English fasttext models from Grave et al. (2018) into a common space. This aesthetic measure will score sentiments on verse level and output their variance on the poem level.

Dividing words into semantic fields can be used as an auxiliary tool in poem analysis in literature studies as it can reveal tensions inside of a poem (c.f Lotman, 1974). By following this notion, we cluster the open class part of speech words based on their cosine similarity within a poem. For this clustering, we use affinity propagation (Frey and Dueck, 2007), which takes a similarity matrix as input and clusters the words based on the matrix. The number of clusters is not fixed and affinity propagation is free to divide the words in as many clusters as necessary.

The clustering aesthetic function looks at the number of clusters in a poem and the average semantic distances of the clusters. The distance between two clusters is calculated by counting a centroid for each cluster based on the word vectors of a cluster and then calculating the cosine distance of the centroids of the clusters. The values output by the aesthetic function will set standards to how semantically cohesive the words have to be with each other, and how distant can their meanings be.

Although words in different clusters might be distant *semantically*, they can be related *pragmatically*. Therefore, we want to reveal possible metaphorical interpretations of a given word in the poem. We represent each semantic cluster found in a poem by a single word. In doing so, we compute the centroid vector of words in each cluster and use the nearest word in the model's vocabulary to the centroid as the topic of the cluster. Thereafter, we iterate over all the possible combinations of having a certain topic as a tenor and another as a vehicle and measure the metaphoricity of the poem with respect to them. We measure that using the two metaphoriticy measurements defined by Alnajjar et al. (2018), one for measuring how a word in the poem relates to both concepts and the other for measuring how related a word is to the vehicle but not to the tenor[5]. The metaphoricity value is then represented by the mean of the two measurements in case both had a positive value, otherwise zero is returned. Using the metaphoricity value assigned to each tenor-vehicle combination, we define two metaphoricity aesthetics 1) the maximum metaphoricity value and 2) the number of metaphorical clusters (i.e. combinations where the metaphoricity value is above zero).

As having many objectives is difficult in practice to handle for the NSGA-II algorithm (see Tanigaki et al., 2014), we group the aesthetic functions into four fitness functions. Sonic (rhyme, alliteration, consonance, assonance, foot and syllable count), semantic (number of clusters and average and maximum distance between the clusters), imagerial (concrete word ratio and variance of sentiment) and metaphorical (the maximum score for metaphoricity and the number of metaphorical words) functions represent the four fitness functions used by the genetic algorithm. These fitness functions sum up the individual aesthetic functions when they are used to score a poem.

4.2 Learning the Aesthetics

We divide our corpus into centuries: the 19th and 20th century. We have two masters learn their aesthetics from either century making them specialized in that century in particular. We first learn weights for the individual aesthetic functions within the higher-level fitness function they belong to. We do this by training four random forest classifiers (Breiman, 2001), one for each of the four

---

[4] http://www.sanakirja.org/

[5] See (Richards, 1936) for more on tenor and vehicle

higher level fitness functions. The classifiers get the features produced by the aesthetic functions belonging to the fitness function in question. The classifiers are trained with the entire corpus to predict true for the desired century and false for other centuries.

The trained classifiers are only used for their weights for each individual feature. These weights are used in the genetic algorithm to multiply the output of each aesthetic function adjusting their importance for the century.

As the weights tell only little about the possible values the aesthetic functions can or should have within one century, we calculate a range of accepted values for each aesthetic function within a century. The 25th percentile of the values is set as the minimum boundary of an accepted value and the 75th percentile as the maximum boundary. If the value output by the aesthetic function is outside of this range, the output value is set to 0.

4.2.1 Master's liking

For the evaluation purposes of the apprentices, it is important to set standards to what is good poetry according to the master. The master likes a poem generated by the apprentice if the poem gets a positive value in each one of the four fitness functions. If any of the values is 0, the master is considered not liking the poems.

4.3 Apprentice

Apprentice is a sequence-to-sequence model that learns to produce creatively altered verses out of verses in existing poetry. To achieve this, we use a BRNN model with a copy attention mechanism by using OpenNMT (Klein et al., 2018). We use the default settings which are two layers for encoding and decoding and general global attention (Luong et al., 2015).

One apprentice is trained from the output of each master, and an additional one from the output of both of the masters. We train the apprentices for 90000 steps to produce poems one verse at a time, from the original poem to the master generated ones. The master for the 19th century produced 11903 poems and the 20th century one 11900 poems out of randomly picked initial poems from the entire corpus. These constitute the training data for the apprentices. The random seed used in training is the same for all apprentices to make intercomparison possible.

5   Results and Evaluation

Evaluation is one of the most important and difficult parts of computational creativity, however it is oftentimes overlooked and conducted in an ad-hoc manner with little to do with the actual problem being modelled (Lamb et al., 2018). In practice this means that a great deal of work is evaluated based on questions and metrics that have not been justified. This practice together with the issue expressed by Veale (2016) that people are ready to read more into the output if it has a suitable linguistic structure regardless of the actual underlying creative intent of the system, are things that should not go unnoticed when evaluating a computationally creative system.

> *Mutta hyökkäykset, jotka kestää sain,*
> *muistot, jotka rakkauden estää,*
> *esiin ilmentyy vihaa kasvattain.*

> But the attacks I was to endure,
> the memories that prevent love,
> emerge amplifying the ire

Above is an example poem output by the master in Finnish followed by its translation in English. The example is of a typical length of a poem produced by the system as the human authored poems were split into stanzas.

5.1   Concepts

The master as a concept is fixed and can only adjust its appreciation, but the apprentice is an entirely new concept that is created from the output of the master. In this section we evaluate the apprentices by evaluating their output by masters' liking. This is done only in an automatic fashion by having all 3 of the apprentices create output for 100 randomly picked poems from the poem corpus.

	master 1800	master 1900
apprentice 1800	28%	33%
apprentice 1900	36%	39%
apprentice both	47%	51%

Table 1: The percentage of the output of the two masters liked

Table 1 shows how many of the poems produced by the different apprentices the masters liked. It is clear from the results that the apprentices did not do too well in terms of learning the century specific aesthetics. Nevertheless, having both of the centuries in the training boosted the results in terms of the two masters liking the poems. This is probably due to the fact of having more training data available.

5.2 Framing and Aesthetics

In order to make it less likely that people read more into the poems than what is there, we evaluate the poems with people based on the framing produced by the system. The main purpose of this evaluation is not to evaluate how *good* the output poems are, but how often the aesthetic functions agree with human judgment. The framing consists of templates that the system fills based on its aesthetic functions. People are asked whether they agree or disagree with the statements expressed in the framing. In addition, people have the possibility of stating that they don't know whether to agree or disagree.

For the evaluation, we sampled 30 poems at random from the poetry generated by the two masters. We printed each poem 5 times, and we divided each set of 30 unique poems into 3 piles of 10 poems with their framing. Each pile was shuffled so that no pile contained exactly the same poems and no pile had the same order for the poems. The shuffling was done to decrease any potential bias introduced by the order of presentation of the poems.

Initially, we recruited 15 people, each one to go through one pile of 10 poems. However, 5 people found the task too time consuming and stopped after evaluating a few poems. The unevaluated poems from these piles were assigned to completely new reviewers. In the end, each unique poem was evaluated 5 times by different people and no individual evaluator evaluated more than 10 poems.

A framing was generated for each poem. The framing followed always the same structure. The first statements relating to rhyming were presented as questions whereas the rest of them were statements. The statements were formed in the following way (translated from Finnish):

1. Do the words written in italics have rhymes (e.g. heikko peikko)?

2. Do the words written in italics have assonance (e.g. **talo sano**)?

3. Do the words written in italics have consonance (e.g. **sakko sokka**)?

4. Does the poem have alliteration within a verse (e.g. **vanha vesi**)?

5. Verse number X and Y have the same meter

6. The poem has X semantic fields: [semantic cluster 1]... and [semantic cluster N]

7. The semantic fields [semantic cluster X] and [semantic cluster Y] are the closest to each other

8. The semantic fields [semantic cluster A] and [semantic cluster B] are the furthest away from each other

9. The following words in the poem [concrete words] are concrete concepts

10. The verse number X is positive

11. The verse number Y is negative

12. The following words in the poem [metaphorical words] can be understood metaphorically

13. The word X has a metaphorical connection to word Y

For the questions on rhyming, the system highlights in italics all the words that have one of the rhyming types. For the meter statement and negative and positive verse statements, random numbers are picked within the range of the length of the poem. For these questions, people agreeing does not produce the highest score, but rather if people's prediction is in line with the prediction of the aesthetic function. Also, if the poem didn't have any metaphorical words, random words were picked for the last two questions. Again, if people disagreed when random words were presented and agreed when actual metaphorical words were presented, the accuracy of the system based on the evaluation would go higher.

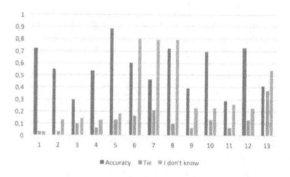

Figure 1: Evaluation results for aesthetics and framing

The accuracy reported in Figure 1 shows how often the prediction (agree/disagree) of the aesthetic functions matches that of the majority of the people out of all the times a majority decision could be reached per poem. The tie shown in the figure shows the percentage of time the statement received an equal number of agreeing and disagreeing opinions from people per poem. The data show by *I don't know* represents the number of times people stated they did not know over all the answers for the statement. Note that this is not calculated per poem but per statement.

The statements related to semantics were the most difficult ones for people to evaluate with around 80% of the time people saying they did not know whether to agree or not. Another difficult statement to judge was the last metaphorical statement including an interpretation for two words being metaphorically connected. This question also included the highest number of ties in people's judgments.

Interestingly, the accuracy was high only for the traditional rhyme types, but lower on the assonance and consonance. Even though our rules can easily and objectively measure the existence of these rhyming types, it is interesting to see that people's judgment deviates from the values output by the aesthetic functions. Especially revealing is the low accuracy on consonance. Our system sees consonance whenever two words have the same consonants in the same positions such as in *jo* (already) and *ja* (and) or *en* (I don't) and *on* (is). Even though these words do exhibit consonance, it seems that people do not find such consonance *perceivable*. This being said, the mere existence of rhyming is not enough, but it should also be perceivable. Just what this perceivability entails is an interesting question left for future research.

For semantics it is difficult to draw any meaningful conclusions as more often than not, people simply did not know whether to agree or not. However, the results do seem promising for the correctness semantic clusters (60 % of the time) and the furthest clusters (72% of the time). At any rate, semantics calls for further qualitative analysis in the future as it seems to be a difficult thing to assess for people.

In the case of imagery, it seems that people agreed on the concreteness 39% of the time, although the score might seem low, it is to remember that all the concrete words were presented as a list in the framing. If even one of the words was not perceived as concrete, people were likely to disagree. Sentiment, on the other hand, resulted in

mixed accuracies; the accuracy for positive sentiment was 69% whereas for negative sentiment the accuracy was 28%. As the sentiment analysis was based on an existing state-of-the-art method, this result is surprising. However, it is very likely the case that negativity in poetry is expressed in a very different way than in other text types. In other words, there is a need for a sentiment annotated corpus consisting of poetry and other literary texts for better predicting the sentiment in poems. All in all, the prediction for concrete words could also benefit from a dataset authored specifically for Finnish.

The accuracy for the metaphorical words was high, 73%. However, the interpretation provided for one of the metaphorical words gave inconclusive results, as people either did not know or had very mixed judgments. This part as well calls for qualitative analysis in the future.

5.3 Expressions

Finally we evaluate the expressions of the master and the apprentice in relation to each other. For this evaluation we treat both of the masters as one, and we evaluate the best apprentice according to the masters' liking. We sample randomly 10 poems from the corpus for which both the master and the apprentice had produced altered poems. We evaluate these poems by asking people which one of the generated poems from the same original one they prefer, that of the master or that of the apprentice. We present the two poems on the same page, shuffling their order for each printout. We also shuffle the order of the poems. We ask 10 people to rate the 20 poems, 10 master generated and 10 apprentice generated ones.

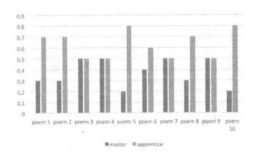

Figure 2: People's preference for each poem

Figure 2 shows the preference of the people per poem. The poetry generated by the apprentice was most often preferred by the judges. The master generated poetry did not reach to a majority in preference for any poem. The interesting question of what happens in the poems that result in a tie in people's preference calls for a future qualitative study to understand better the phenomenon of the evaluation.

6 Conclusions

We have shown our novel method for generating poetry in Finnish. With the help of the FACE model, we were able to conduct evaluation on the aesthetics and framing that was revealing of the shortcomings of our system. Framing made it possible to assess the core functionality better by minimizing the room for people reading more into the poem than what was there. Having the option for people to say that they do not know rather than forcing them to either agree or disagree revealed the difficulty of assessing semantics and metaphors even for people. We propose for the future to conduct evaluation on such high level features of language on a qualitative fashion to better understand how people perceive these in generated poetry.

As a vast majority of the NLP research focuses on English, we had to deal with the practical issue of the scarce annotated resources for Finnish to capture the high level features such as concreteness, sentiment and metaphor. As a result we ended up developing useful resources for the aesthetic functions which we have made publicly available on Github[6].

References

Rodrigo Agerri, Montse Cuadros, Sean Gaines, and German Rigau. 2013. Opener: Open polarity enhanced named entity recognition. *Procesamiento del Lenguaje Natural*, (51).

Khalid Alnajjar, Hadaytullah Hadaytullah, and Hannu Toivonen. 2018. "Talent, Skill and Support." A method for automatic creation of slogans. In *Proceedings of the 9th International Conference on Computational Creativity (ICCC 2018)*, pages 88–95, Salamanca, Spain. Association for Computational Creativity.

Khalid Alnajjar and Mika Hämäläinen. 2018. A master-apprentice approach to automatic creation of culturally satirical movie titles. In *Proceedings of the 11th International Conference on Natural Language Generation*, pages 274–283.

Leo Breiman. 2001. Random forests. *Machine learning*, 45(1):5–32.

Marc Brysbaert, Amy Beth Warriner, and Victor Kuperman. 2014. Concreteness ratings for 40 thousand generally known english word lemmas. *Behavior research methods*, 46(3):904–911.

Janet Burroway. 2007. *Imaginative Writing: The Elements of Craft*. Pearson.

David J Chalmers. 1995. Absent qualia, fading qualia, dancing qualia. *Conscious experience*, pages 309–328.

John William Charnley, Alison Pease, and Simon Colton. 2012. On the notion of framing in computational creativity. In *ICCC*, pages 77–81.

Simon Colton, John William Charnley, and Alison Pease. 2011. Computational creativity theory: The FACE and IDEA descriptive models. In *ICCC*, pages 90–95.

Simon Colton, Jacob Goodwin, and Tony Veale. 2012. Full-FACE poetry generation. In *ICCC*, pages 95–102.

Michael Cook, Simon Colton, Alison Pease, and Maria Theresa Llano. 2019. Framing in computational creativity – a survey and taxonomy. In *The proceedings of the tenth international conference on computational creativity*, pages 156–163.

K. Deb, A. Pratap, S. Agarwal, and T. Meyarivan. 2002. A fast and elitist multiobjective genetic algorithm: Nsga-ii. *Trans. Evol. Comp*, 6(2):182–197.

Yanlin Feng and Xiaojun Wan. 2019. Learning bilingual sentiment-specific word embeddings without cross-lingual supervision. In *Proceedings of the 2019 Conference of the North American Chapter of the Association for Computational Linguistics: Human Language Technologies, Volume 1 (Long and Short Papers)*, pages 420–429, Minneapolis, Minnesota. Association for Computational Linguistics.

Brendan J Frey and Delbert Dueck. 2007. Clustering by passing messages between data points. *science*, 315(5814):972–976.

Pablo Gervás. 2001. An expert system for the composition of formal Spanish poetry. In *Applications and Innovations in Intelligent Systems VIII*, pages 19–32. Springer.

Edouard Grave, Piotr Bojanowski, Prakhar Gupta, Armand Joulin, and Tomas Mikolov. 2018. Learning word vectors for 157 languages. In *Proceedings of the International Conference on Language Resources and Evaluation (LREC 2018)*.

Mika Hämäläinen. 2018. Harnessing NLG to create Finnish poetry automatically. In *Proceedings of the Ninth International Conference on Computational Creativity*, pages 9–15.

Mika Hämäläinen. 2019. UralicNLP: An NLP library for Uralic languages. *Journal of Open Source Software*, 4(37):1345.

---

[6]https://github.com/mikahama/finmeter

Mika Hämäläinen and Jack Rueter. 2018. Development of an Open Source Natural Language Generation Tool for Finnish. In *Proceedings of the Fourth International Workshop on Computational Linguistics for Uralic Languages*, pages 51–58.

Katri Haverinen, Jenna Nyblom, Timo Viljanen, Veronika Laippala, Samuel Kohonen, Anna Missilä, Stina Ojala, Tapio Salakoski, and Filip Ginter. 2014. Building the essential resources for Finnish: the Turku dependency treebank. *Language Resources and Evaluation*, 48(3):493–531.

Kyle E. Jennings. 2010. Developing Creativity: Artificial Barriers in Artificial Intelligence. *Minds and Machines*, 20(4):489–501.

Anna Jordanous. 2012. A standardised procedure for evaluating creative systems: Computational creativity evaluation based on what it is to be creative. *Cognitive Computation*, 4(3):246–279.

Tuomas Juntunen. 2012. Kirjallisuudentutkimus. In *Genreanalyysi: tekstilajitutkimuksen käsikirja*, pages 528—536.

Jenna Kanerva, Juhani Luotolahti, Veronika Laippala, and Filip Ginter. 2014. Syntactic n-gram collection from a large-scale corpus of internet Finnish. In *Human Language Technologies-The Baltic Perspective: Proceedings of the Sixth International Conference Baltic HLT*, volume 268, pages 184–191.

Mervi Kantokorpi, Lyytikäinen Pirjo, and Viikari Auli. 1990. *Runousopin perusteet*. Gaudeamus.

Justine Kao and Dan Jurafsky. 2012. A computational analysis of style, affect, and imagery in contemporary poetry. In *Proceedings of the NAACL-HLT 2012 Workshop on Computational Linguistics for Literature*, pages 8–17.

Guillaume Klein, Yoon Kim, Yuntian Deng, Vincent Nguyen, Jean Senellart, and Alexander Rush. 2018. OpenNMT: Neural machine translation toolkit. In *Proceedings of the 13th Conference of the Association for Machine Translation in the Americas (Volume 1: Research Papers)*, pages 177–184, Boston, MA. Association for Machine Translation in the Americas.

Carolyn Lamb and Daniel G. Brown. 2019. TwitSong 3.0: towards semantic revisions in computational poetry. In *Proceedings of the Tenth International Conference on Computational Creativity*, pages 212–219.

Carolyn Lamb, Daniel G Brown, and Charles LA Clarke. 2018. Evaluating computational creativity: An interdisciplinary tutorial. *ACM Computing Surveys (CSUR)*, 51(2):28.

Juntao Li, Yan Song, Haisong Zhang, Dongmin Chen, Shuming Shi, Dongyan Zhao, and Rui Yan. 2018. Generating classical Chinese poems via conditional variational autoencoder and adversarial training.

In *Proceedings of the 2018 Conference on Empirical Methods in Natural Language Processing*, pages 3890–3900, Brussels, Belgium. Association for Computational Linguistics.

Juri Lotman. 1974. *Den poetiska texten*. Stockholm.

Minh-Thang Luong, Hieu Pham, and Christopher D Manning. 2015. Effective approaches to attention-based neural machine translation. *arXiv preprint arXiv:1508.04025*.

Tomas Mikolov, Ilya Sutskever, Kai Chen, Greg S Corrado, and Jeff Dean. 2013. Distributed representations of words and phrases and their compositionality. In *Advances in neural information processing systems*, pages 3111–3119.

Joanna Misztal and Bipin Indurkhya. 2014. Poetry generation system with an emotional personality. In *ICCC*, pages 72–81.

Hugo Gonçalo Oliveira. 2017. A survey on intelligent poetry generation: Languages, features, techniques, reutilisation and evaluation. In *Proceedings of the 10th International Conference on Natural Language Generation*, pages 11–20, Santiago de Compostela, Spain. Association for Computational Linguistics.

Hugo Gonçalo Oliveira, Raquel Hervás, Alberto Díaz, and Pablo Gervás. 2017. Multilingual extension and evaluation of a poetry generator. *Natural Language Engineering*, 23(6):929–967.

Tommi A Pirinen, Inari Listenmaa, Ryan Johnson, Francis M. Tyers, and Juha Kuokkala. 2017. Open morphology of finnish. LINDAT/CLARIN digital library at the Institute of Formal and Applied Linguistics, Charles University.

Ivor Armstrong Richards. 1936. *The Philosophy of Rhetoric*. Oxford University Press, London, United Kingdom.

Yuki Tanigaki, Kaname Narukawa, Yusuke Nojima, and Hisao Ishibuch. 2014. Preference-based nsga-ii for many-objective knapsack problems. In *2014 Joint 7th International Conference on Soft Computing and Intelligent Systems (SCIS) and 15th International Symposium on Advanced Intelligent Systems (ISIS)*, pages 637–642. IEEE.

Jukka Toivanen, Hannu Toivonen, Alessandro Valitutti, and Oskar Gross. 2012. Corpus-Based Generation of Content and Form in Poetry. In *Proceedings of the Third International Conference on Computational Creativity*.

Tony Veale. 2016. The shape of tweets to come: automating language play in social networks. *Multiple Perspectives on Language Play. Mouton De Gruyter, Language Play and Creativity series*, pages 73–92.

Ping Xiao, Khalid Alnajjar, Mark Granroth-Wilding, Kathleen Agres, and Hannu Toivonen. 2016.

Meta4meaning: Automatic metaphor interpretation using corpus-derived word associations. In *Proceedings of the 7th International Conference on Computational Creativity (ICCC 2016)*, Paris, France. Sony CSL, Sony CSL.

Cheng Yang, Maosong Sun, Xiaoyuan Yi, and Wenhao Li. 2018. Stylistic Chinese poetry generation via unsupervised style disentanglement. In *Proceedings of the 2018 Conference on Empirical Methods in Natural Language Processing*, pages 3960–3969, Brussels, Belgium. Association for Computational Linguistics.

Xiaoyuan Yi, Maosong Sun, Ruoyu Li, and Wenhao Li. 2018. Automatic poetry generation with mutual reinforcement learning. In *Proceedings of the 2018 Conference on Empirical Methods in Natural Language Processing*, pages 3143–3153, Brussels, Belgium. Association for Computational Linguistics.

Co-Operation as an Asymmetric Form of Human-Computer Creativity. Case: Peace Machine

Mika Hämäläinen
Department of Digital Humanities
University of Helsinki
mika.hamalainen@helsinki.fi

Timo Honkela
Department of Digital Humanities
University of Helsinki
timo.honkela@helsinki.fi

Abstract

This theoretical paper identifies a need for a definition of asymmetric co-creativity where creativity is expected from the computational agent but not from the human user. Our co-operative creativity framework takes into account that the computational agent has a message to convey in a co-operative fashion, which introduces a trade-off on how creative the computer can be. The requirements of co-operation are identified from an interdisciplinary point of view. We divide co-operative creativity in *message creativity, contextual creativity* and *communicative creativity*. Finally these notions are applied in the context of the Peace Machine system concept.

1 Introduction

When we say something in a language, we say it to communicate something. Every utterance we say has a meaning behind it, a *message* we want to convey to others. This is true not only in everyday conversation, but in any act of language use, no matter the medium, whether it was spoken, written, signed etc.

For computationally creative systems, exhibiting linguistic creativity, expressing a message is not a requirement. In fact, just generating a linguistic realization, a surface form, is challenging enough and is considered of a merit.

The situation becomes more difficult when *mere surface generation*, i.e. producing natural language without a message, is not enough. When a system has to generate a creative poem that expresses a complete message or has to make a meaning conveying contribution to a conversation. It is often the case that a computationally creative system is not fully aware of the meaning its creations convey, but rather rely on people to pour their understanding of the world into the creative artifact and perceive creativity in it.

In this paper, we focus on co-operative creativity with the focus on dialog systems. We are not greatly interested in purely generative dialog systems that serve more for chitchat. Instead, we focus on goal-oriented dialog systems that have a clear message they need to convey, such as a price or available times, and the role of computational creativity in encapsulating their message in a creative form.

Creative behavior consisting of a human and a computer is called co-creativity. In the following section, we start by discussing this notion and why it is insufficient for modelling our task. In the following sections, we take an interdisciplinary view on what co-operation means and formulate a creative framework based on these notions. Finally we show a more concrete way of using our framework by applying it on the Peace Machine concept.

In the field of computational creativity, working with a definition for creativity plays a crucial role in evaluation of a creative system (Jordanous, 2012; Alnajjar and Hämäläinen, 2018). While a myriad of more abstract level theories on computational creativity have been elaborated in the past (Colton, 2008; Wiggins, 2006; Colton et al., 2011), our work aims to develop a theoretical framework to a more concrete problem of creative dialog generation.

2 Co-Creativity

In this section, we describe some of the existing definitions of human computer co-creativity as the co-creativity paradigm is closest to our case.

Co-creativity can be divided into four categories as identified by Lubart (2005). The computer can act as a *nanny* to a person guiding and motivating him in the creative task, where as if the computer acts as a *coach*, it will more actively help the

Proceedings of the 1st Workshop on NLP for Conversational AI, pages 42–50
Florence, Italy, August 1, 2019. ©2019 Association for Computational Linguistics

creative person to explore new ways of thinking by educating them about different creativity techniques. In a *pen-pal* scenario, the computer helps a creative individual in communicating ideas with others. Finally, the computer can be a *colleague* in which case humans and computers are in a creative dialogue taking turns in forming a creative artefact.

Davis (2013) identifies a gap between the AI research focusing on computational creativity and HCI (human-computer interaction) research focusing on creativity support tools. He argues that co-creativity can narrow this gap. Creativity is seen as an emergent phenomenon from the interactions of a human and a computer. The interactions are collaborative and both parties influence on each other.

In mixed initiative co-creativity (Yannakakis et al., 2014), both the computer and a human user take an active role in contributing to solving a creative problem, although, not necessarily to the same extent. This differs from turn-based collaboration between the two parties and from the computer being merely a supportive tool, as the both parties are actively creative.

In a recent study outlining evaluation of co-creativity (Karimi et al., 2018), the concept of co-creativity is defined as an interaction involving at least one AI agent and one human. They act based on the creative response of the other party and their own understanding of creativity.

The current definitions of co-creativity always expect the presence of human creativity in addition to computational creativity or computer assisted creativity. However, a co-operation setting does not require creativity at all, and if the computational agent is creative, it does not mean that there has to be human creativity present at the same time.

3 Co-Operation

Co-operative creativity requires the computer to exhibit creativity in its way of communication. However, creativity is not a requirement for the human user. Even though dialogue itself can be seen as an interplay between two or more parties forming an ephemeral creative artefact of its own, we want to clearly distinguish co-operative creativity from co-creativity. Therefore, we are not looking at dialogue as a creative artefact but rather how creativity can take place one-sidedly on the level of utterances.

3.1 Communicative-Creative Trade off

The purpose of a dialogue system, whether it is made for chitchat or to answer queries, is always to co-operate with a human. Co-operation can thus, in its simplest form, be contributing to the conversation in a meaningful way to keep the conversation on going.

The rules of conversation are governed by linguistic, cognitive and social mechanisms that have to be followed, and they set limitations for creativity. For instance, a dialogue system for booking movie tickets can deliver a very uncreative communicative answer stating just the name of the movie and its showtime or on the other extreme of creativity, answering by a riddle.

We argue that the co-operative nature of conversation, where creativity is only expected from the computer, not from the human, and where a certain communicative function has to be filled in accordance to higher level rules of conversation, has to balance in between creativity and predictability.

3.2 Communication in Pragmatics

The field of pragmatics has been studying meaning in its context for multiple decades. In this section, we will explain the key pragmatic theories in understanding conversation and meaning of utterances.

Grice (1975) famously defined four maxims for co-operative principle of communication: manner, quality, quantity and relevance. Through these maxims, we can identify linguistic rules that a machine should follow in order to be converse in a co-operative fashion.

The maxim of manner means that the communication is conducted in an orderly and unambiguous fashion. The maxim of quality refers to the truthfulness of the utterance. The speaker shall not say anything he believes to be false.

If there is just enough information communicated in an utterance, the maxim of quantity is followed. This means that both communicating too little or too much is against this maxim. The last maxim, namely that of relevance, requires the utterance to be contextually related and not off topic.

When it comes to the function of utterances, i.e. their relation to the surrounding world, we can use Searle's speech acts (Searle, 1969) (cf. Nonaka, 1994; Rus et al., 2012). According to this theory, all utterances are either representative, expressive, declarative, commissive or directive.

Representative and expressive are close to each other in a communicative function. The former states something factual about the surrounding reality outside of the speaker, where as the latter is a statement about the internal state, such as the emotion, of the speaker.

Directive speech acts are commands, i.e. their intention is to make someone else perform an action. Commissive speech acts have a similar function as they are promises, in their case the speaker is the one who is going to perform the action. Declarative speech acts are, by their definition, supposed to change the surrounding world. An example of such a speech act is sentencing someone guilty of a crime.

It is important to note that the surface form of an utterance does not dictate the speech act it is used to perform, but rather its contextualization plays an important role. For instance, a prayer is an expressive speech act even though on the surface it might seem as a directive speech act. This interplay between the context and the words themselves opens up a great potential for creativity.

3.3 Socio-Cognitive Views

In cognitive science, the concept of scripts (cf. Bower et al., 1979) can be used in a higher level to explain communication. In day-to-day life, our brains rely on heuristics when processing information. This helps us perform tasks in a cognitively less intensive fashion. Scripts store learned patterns of behaviour and outcome of different situations. For instance, paying for groceries follows a well defined script: stand in a line waiting for your turn, place the items on the belt, pay and go packing. By following this script, we do not have to figure out how to pay for our groceries every time we need to buy food. It is to be noted, though, that the scripts vary according to geographical and cultural areas. The script for visiting a grocery store or bank is different, e.g., in the USA, different parts of Europe or China.

A higher level theory of the same phenomenon is the one presented by Goffman (1959). According to his view, social life is assimilated to a theater play, where every participant is supposed to play their own role. In the level of interaction, the focus of his interest is in maintaining face. The common goal of the interlocutors in a conversation is to maintain their own social face and those of the other participants.

3.4 Usability and Design

When we are dealing with dialogue systems, we cannot overlook the fact that we are inherently dealing with a user interface. In the fields of usability and design, the problem of communication has been dealt with from the human-computer interaction point of view.

A simple heuristic in usability for assessing a user interface is to look at the mental and physical effort (cf. Komogortsev et al., 2009) required to perform a task. For dialogue systems, physical effort can be calculated by how many queries the user has to perform to complete a given task. Mental effort refers to all cognitively demanding tasks such as how much information the user has to gather and memorize from different parts of the interface. Thus a dialogue system listing all the possible flights with all the details when requested would have low requirement for physical effort, but would be cognitively intensive as the user would have to memorize every flight he finds suitable.

Maybe a more intriguing concept in design is that of elegance (cf. White 2011). An elegant design communicates the intended message fully with as little as possible. The communication in a message can be divided in two: in denotation and connotation. Where denotation is the pure information content of the message, connotation is more in the way the message is communicated - in the emotional response it evokes.

3.5 Synthesis

In the previous sections, we have dedicated much room for describing the theories from different disciplines that in their core, are dealing with the very same phenomenon - communication. This section is dedicated into putting the theories together to form an interdisciplinary framework for a dialog system that is independent of the technical realization or creativity at this point.

We take elegance and script as higher level concepts as they are on the highest level of abstraction. Reflecting these in terms of the co-operative principle, i.e. the maxims, we can notice that elegance is closely related to the maxims of quantity and quality. As the requirement of elegance is to express the message as fully as possible (quality) with as little as possible (quantity), an elegant utterance needs to fulfill these two maxims.

Scripts are most strongly related to the maxims of manner and relevance. As scripts give us behavioral patterns to follow in different situations, they govern the manner in which we are expected to express ourselves. The behavioral patterns also entail what is relevant to say in which situation.

We place the usability terms on the lowest level in our synthesized model of co-operation, as they are meant to assess a concrete human-computer interaction scenario. Physical effort is linked mostly to the maxims of quantity and relevance. A dialogue system providing too little information will force the user to ask for more details, which increases the amount of physical effort. This is true also in the case of non-relevant information, which provokes more queries by the user to reach to a relevant answer.

The maxim of quantity relates to mental effort as well. Too much information will force the user to store it in his memory, which increases the mental effort. Another maxim affecting on mental effort is that of manner. If the information is not presented in an orderly manner, it makes it more difficult for the user to gather the important bits of information into a cohesive whole.

Coming back to the highest level concepts, elegance and script, a bridge needs to be built to connect them. We argue that they are connected through the context in which the conversation takes place. The context triggers a script, but it also changes the meaning of what is elegant. Talking with a person who knows a great deal about the topic of the conversation requires less words to communicate the message whereas more explaining is in order for a person new to the topic.

The context is also dictated by the *role* one is expected to *play* in the social situation. Therefore Goffman's theory is a part of the contextual bridge linking the two highest level concepts. We also introduce a mental model of the interlocutor as a part of the context as it has been proven evident by the previous discussion, that the maxims depend on the interlocutor as well. Furthermore, the conversation develops in time, which means that the prior utterances are also building the current context.

Now that we have synthesized what co-operative conversation requires, it is time to add the remaining notions into the model. No conversation can take place meaningfully if there is no

message to be conveyed by the words of an utterance. This message can be divided into its denotative and connotative function. How the message can be conveyed is limited by the speech acts, and they function as a gate to the conversation.

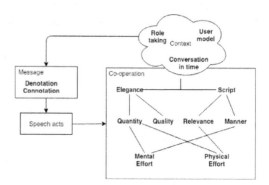

Figure 1: Model of co-operation

Figure 1 depicts the model described in this section. This model does not take creativity into account, but rather describes the requirements of co-operation and their inter-dependencies. The context is connected back into the message component as it affects on the next utterance of the conversation.

4 Co-Operative Creativity

In the previous section, we identified three main components of a co-operative dialogue system: message (including speech acts), context and co-operation , which correspond to *message*, *contextual* and *communicative creativity* respectively. In this section, we shed light into how computational creativity can manifest itself without jeopardizing the strict requirement of co-operation.

4.1 Message Creativity

In a co-operative setting, there is a limitation to what can be communicated so that it is still relevant for the conversation. The limitation can be very strict like in the case of a dialogue system selling tickets or lenient as in the case of chitchat.

4.1.1 Creativity in Denotation

Even if the set of possible denotations was limited, there is room for creativity in finding something else to communicate that is still co-operative. For example, *glass is half full* and *glass is half empty* communicate about the same phenomenon, yet their denotations are different. Thus, finding a creative point of view to communicate about the same phenomenon is a way of altering the denotation of the message without making it non-cooperative.

In a more lenient setting, the context of the message can be explored to find a way to communicate a denotation that still contributes to the co-operativity. This could, for instance, be a change of topic or a message provoking an emotional change such as a joke.

4.1.2 Creativity in Connotation

Even if the denotation of a message was fully fixed, for example, if the system has to communicate the price of a movie ticket and cannot communicate any other denotation to avoid risking co-operativity, connotation opens up more room for creativity.

Connotation can be altered as easily as by the choice of words or by a structural change. Consider for example the following sentences *An appointment for vaccination has been reserved for Monday* and *You will get your shot on Monday*. Both of them communicate the same denotation, but their connotation is different. The first sentence sounds more official and establishes social distance where as the latter is more casual in style.

4.1.3 Exploiting Speech Acts

Speech acts are more abstract in nature than any linguistic form, and thus speech acts themselves do not offer much room for creativity. However, understanding that certain surface realizations are most closely attached to certain speech acts, opens up a window for creativity.

I like strawberries is seemingly an expressive speech act; the person tries to communicate about his liking of strawberries. However, the actual speech act might be directive *give me strawberries* or commissive *I will buy strawberries*, depending on the context. Therefore mixing and matching speech acts with non-typical surface forms that still communicate the message is an exploitable possibility of computational creativity.

4.2 Contextual Creativity

The context has a huge effect on how communicated messages are understood. As we have seen throughout this paper, words can mean different things in different contexts. A context also sets limits to what can be said and how it should be said.

4.2.1 User Adaptation

Knowing the user and establishing trust with him gives more freedom for creative behavior. Even in tightly scripted situations, if the user is known well, the communication can deviate more from the script without it damaging the co-operation.

A semantic model that has been learned from the user in question could be used to creatively adapt a message to the user's own vocabulary. If for example the user hates *frozen yogurt* a flight connection with tediously long layovers could be communicated as *a frozen yogurt route*.

A creatively expressed message has a higher risk to not being understood. A good user model can then provide a way of assessing whether a creative communication solution will be understood as intended or not.

4.2.2 Role Identification

If we look at communication from the perspective of role-taking, a great source of creativity can come from identifying the possible roles supported by the context and picking the one that gives the greatest freedom in expression.

Role identification from user perspective, especially if there are many human users, can contribute to the creative freedom. If there are more than one possible roles the users can take, changing their role to one that offers more freedom of creativity can be of a benefit. The roles can be changed by communicative means.

4.2.3 Time Perspective

Planning the flow of the conversation ahead doing constant predictions is a potential way of shifting the context towards one that has more room for creativity. The planning itself can also be a creative process where the conversation will take unexpected turns that still contribute to co-operation.

Just as much as predicting the future can be a creative process, knowing the past can be used creatively as well. This is not limited to creative comebacks to what the user has said, but also can mean re-interpretation of what has been said before. Language is ambiguous and this fact can be celebrated by reusing bits of the conversation form the past in the new current context.

4.3 Communicative Creativity

The co-operation section in Figure 1 is probably the part that limits creativity the most. Maxims and the other components they relate to set rules to how one is supposed to communicate in order to do it in a co-operative fashion. However, there is room for creativity even with these tight rules.

4.3.1 Script Selection

In a conversation situation, there might be multiple social scripts to choose from. Picking a non-typical, but yet contextually fitting script can make it possible to find new creative solutions in the conversation.

As scripts are not predefined hand-written rules, but rather learned behavioral patterns, scripts offer flexibility in changing them. Identifying how to change a script, or how to go outside of one, in a way that it does not startle the interlocutor, is a task requiring creativity.

4.3.2 Adjustment of Elegance

Optimizing for elegance is probably too limiting for creativity and not an interesting way to go about creativity in conversation. The question should be what is elegant enough, and what is expected to be communicated. A longer message might be seen inelegant as it uses too many words to communicate a message, if we are only interested in the denotation. However, the additional length might contribute to connotation.

Making justified statements about elegance requires a definition of what is communicated, the message itself. This tells what is expected to be communicated, which then in its turn, makes it possible to assess the elegance of the utterance.

4.3.3 Informed Deviation from Maxims

Maxims are a part of co-operative principle and thus by definition they are tailored towards co-operative conversation. However, they are highly contextual and therefore what is enough, relevant and so on is a matter of the context in which an utterance occurs.

A system seeking to deviate from the maxims and still maintain co-operativity in the communication needs to be able to assess the effect of such a deviation in a reasoned way. For example, if the goal is to make the user think and ask questions, communicating a bit too little or increasing ambiguity might be useful.

A seemingly irrelevant communication can be useful if the communication is later contextualized and made relevant for the initial conversation topic. Sometimes telling anecdotes or giving analogous examples might seem irrelevant to the in-terlocutor, but later in the conversation they can prove to be helpful in understanding the problem from another perspective.

The maxim of quality relates to truthfulness of the utterance. Expressing something that is clearly untrue can be a way of expressing the opposite meaning in a sarcastic fashion (cf. Hämäläinen, 2016). If the sarcasm is understood correctly by the user, the communication can still be co-operative, even though on the surface it appears to be insincere.

5 The Context of Peace Machine

Peace Machine (Honkela, 2017) is a concept on how to use different parts of Artificial Intelligence (AI) to promote peaceful conditions in the world. This highly ambitious objective may sound unrealistic at first. It is to be remembered, though, that the range of AI technologies that have considerable impact in various domains is wide and increasing.

The Peace Machine concept consists of three main areas. The question is not about one system but a number of different applications and systems. The three main areas considered are (1) Improved communication, (2) Understanding emotions, and (3) Improving societal conditions.

5.1 Co-Operative Creativity in Peace Machine

In the following, the Peace Machine concept is considered from the point of view of Co-Operative Creativity defined and described in this paper. Peace Machine serves as a general application context for the theoretical work presented in this paper and its components can be studies in the communicative framework presented in this paper.

5.2 Message Creativity

The objective of Peace Machine is to help the user of a component of the system use and learn communicative acts that help him navigate in the conversational space in a peaceful and constructive manner or understand one's own or others' emotions in a constructive way. To be successful in this task, the system must be able to express itself in a creative manner when necessary. The user may need help in seeing matters from a novel point of view or in understanding the current situation beyond the limits of the conceptual system that he may have available. This help may be reached, for instance, with the use of metaphor.

5.2.1 Creativity in Denotation

The topic of conversation may be guided into areas in which, for instance, the risk of emotional outbursts are lowered. The creativity of the system would lie in the ability to guide the topics of the conversation even when the overall communicative goal remains the same. One opportunity is to find a path in the conversation that minimizes unintended choice of topics or expressions that might endanger the overall goal. It is known from practical experience in peace negotiations that the use of a poorly chosen single word or theme may jeopardize the whole process. Here it is to be remembered that Peace Machine is not focusing on peace negotiations between nations or other such organizations but between any two or more people.

5.2.2 Creativity in Connotation

In Peace Machine, consideration of the connotation is very important. When the aim is to reach peaceful and constructive communication, expressions that have negative connotations should be avoided. In a conversation between two people, the system may help the persons to avoid expressions that hurt other's emotions or the ground of his identity. In many cultures it is important to take social aspects into account. Depending on the relationship between the people, their status and cultural background, the expressions that are appropriate in one situation may be quite the opposite in another. For instance, the same content can be expressed in two quite different ways regarding the style: *Let's have a meeting tomorrow!* or *May I have the honor to ask your presence in meeting in the near future, potentially already tomorrow?*.

5.2.3 Exploiting Speech Acts

Useful computational creativity that helps people through potentially problematic communication can take place through suitable choices regarding speech acts. In a homely context, there is a clear difference between the expressions *Take out the trash bin* and *The trash bin is quite smelly*. The intention can be considered to be the same in both cases but the emotional outcome may be quite different. Whether illocutionary, perlocutionary, propositional or utterance act should be chosen depends on multiple factors that concern the persons involved, their background, history of the communication and the broader context. At

the present moment, it is still difficult to take into account the non-linguistic context in human-like manner. It is, however, good to keep in mind that persons may interpret the non-linguist or implicit context in a different way especially if they, for instance, have different education or cultural background (cf. Anderson and Shifrin, 2017).

5.3 Contextual Creativity

In Peace Machine, as in any general purpose system, the challenge of world knowledge and the huge complexity of the contexts that a system may encounter is a great challenge as well as an opportunity. This could be an indirect or direct access to the context. Here indirect refers to the use of language and the direct refers to use of perceptual senses. The underlying matters have been a subject to philosophical debates for very long time (cf. Gärdenfors, 2000; Von Foerster, 2007; Bundgaard, 2010) and it is not possible to cover this theme here. From the point of view of Peace Machine, the room for computational creativity is extensive and given broad range of opportunities. In building peace one possible approach is to choose the topics and dimensions suitably. For instance, the choice can help the discussants feel safe and secure. A useful notion is the division into foreground and background that is used in cognitive linguistics (Langacker, 2008). Sometimes it may be useful and constructive to start conversational from the background and gradually proceed into the foreground. The creative system may help humans in finding such conversational routes.

5.3.1 User Adaptation

In the above discussion referring to context, the aspect of subjectivity was briefly brought up. In addition to their experiences, values, preferences and identity, people are also different regarding their linguistic and conceptual systems. We do not know the same set of words and their meanings and we even have different interpretations of words and expressions. The words "fair" or "beautiful" refer to different things, which should be obvious, but more difficult to measure than comparing the limits or distributions of interpretation of color "orange" or whether some product is "expensive". In Peace Machine, this theme is very important as it has been pointed out that misunderstanding is a very common phenomenon that has wide practical consequences. Creative user adaptation on language and conceptual systems is presented as a potentially important means to serve a basis for highly improved communication. This is a hypotheses that needs to be tested in various kinds of settings.

5.3.2 Role Identification

A machine, the purpose of which is to help people understand one another, can take up different roles in a communicative setting. In a situation of conflict, a suitable role might be that of a mediator while some situations require a more active leader-like role from the machine. This gives the machine a spectrum of roles from the passive to active to choose from.

5.3.3 Time Perspective

Helping people understand one another is a task with a persuasive goal. This persuasion requires planning, and the creative outcomes of the flow of the conversation have to be taken into account by the system.

With an aim for peace, Peace Machine should be able to take turns in the conversation that get the interlocutor off guard. In an extremely polarized setting, the two opposing parties are biased towards not being open towards the other party's opinions. A persuasion technique such as this one requires creative planning.

5.4 Communicative Creativity for Peace Machine

In the following, we consider how to communicate in a co-operative fashion while using the Peace Machine system.

5.4.1 Script Selection

Useful scripts to promote mutual understanding and respect can be learned based on large corpora of conversations. The real world variety of contexts makes its useful to apply creative solutions when the corpus-based solution does not provide close enough solution. Two or more solutions may be merged.

5.4.2 Adjustment of Elegance

Elegance is seemingly an important criterion regarding Peace Machine. The system should communicate in such a manner that it matches with the user's linguistic expectations and situation-specific needs. Too short and ambiguous message may be considered impolite or rude. Equally well, a message too long may be considered uninteresting or impolite. The Peace Machine system

component can be used to train a person to handle potentially troublesome situations, during the conversation with someone else, or to help by analyzing an earlier conversation.

5.4.3 Informed Deviation from Maxims

From the point of view of the Peace Machine concept and system use, among the Grice's (1975) four maxims for co-operative principle of communication, manner, quality, quantity and relevance, can be used to judge potential usefulness of breaking these rules in a creative way. Regarding manner, the system may guide a person to be unclear or ambiguous in order to give room for alternative helpful interpretations or ideas, or to point out that the terminology and conceptual space may be such that meaning negotiation would be useful regarding the conversational situation at hand. The initial problem may help in understanding that the basis is not the same regarding the meaning of some key term in the conversation.

Changing the topic in the middle of a conversation and not being relevant may be a means to create a possibility to escape a problematic conversational situation. This approach should be used with care because it may lead into unintended consequences. For instance, the expression may be interpreted as an insult rather than as, for instance, humorous break to a heated discussion.

6 Conclusions

This paper has identified a need for theoretical framework for asymmetric human-computer creativity, where, for the first time, the computer is the only party with a requirement for creativity. Thus our initial framework fills a theoretical void in the field.

In this paper we have outlined from an interdisciplinary point of view what the requirements are for a co-operative conversation. Based on this definition, we have identified three different kinds of creativity in a co-operative setting: message, contextual and conversational creativity.

Furthermore, we have highlighted the importance of having a message to convey creatively. This makes a clear distinction with the creative systems that generate language without a need to communicate a certain idea, a message. Due to the nature of dialogue systems that are meant to aid users reach their goal, this need for a message cannot be ignored.

References

Khalid Alnajjar and Mika Hämäläinen. 2018. A Master-Apprentice Approach to Automatic Creation of Culturally Satirical Movie Titles. In *Proceedings of the 11th International Conference on Natural Language Generation (INLG)*, pages 274—283.

Richard C Anderson and Zohara Shifrin. 2017. The meaning of words in context. In *Theoretical issues in reading comprehension*, pages 331–348. Routledge.

Gordon H Bower, John B Black, and Terrence J Turner. 1979. Scripts in memory for text. *Cognitive Psychology*, 11(2):177 – 220.

Peer F Bundgaard. 2010. Husserl and language. In *Handbook of phenomenology and cognitive science*, pages 368–399. Springer.

Simon Colton. 2008. Creativity Versus the Perception of Creativity in Computational Systems. In *AAAI Spring Symposium: Creative Intelligent Systems*, Technical Report SS-08-03, pages 14—20, Stanford, California, USA.

Simon Colton, John William Charnley, and Alison Pease. 2011. Computational creativity theory: The face and idea descriptive models. In *ICCC*, pages 90–95.

Nicholas Davis. 2013. Human-computer co-creativity: Blending human and computational creativity. In *Ninth Artificial Intelligence and Interactive Digital Entertainment Conference*.

Erving Goffman. 1959. *The Presentation of Self in Everyday Life*. University of Edinburgh Social Sciences Research Centre.

H Paul Grice. 1975. Logic and conversation. *1975*, pages 41–58.

Peter Gärdenfors. 2000. *Conceptual Spaces: The Geometry of Thought*. MIT Press, Cambridge, MA, USA.

Mika Hämäläinen. 2016. Reconocimiento automático del sarcasmo - ¡Esto va a funcionar bien! Master's thesis, University of Helsinki, Finland. URN:NBN:fi:hulib-201606011945.

Timo Honkela. 2017. *Rauhankone. Tekoälytutkijan testamentti*. Gaudeamus.

Anna Jordanous. 2012. A standardised procedure for evaluating creative systems: Computational creativity evaluation based on what it is to be creative. *Cognitive Computation*, 4(3):246–279.

Pegah Karimi, Kazjon Grace, Mary Lou Maher, and Nicholas Davis. 2018. Evaluating creativity in computational co-creative systems. In *The Proceedings of the Ninth International Conference on Computational Creativity, ICCC*.

O Komogortsev, Carl J Mueller, Dan Tamir, and Liam Feldman. 2009. An effort based model of software usability. In *2009 International Conference on Software Engineering Theory and Practice (SETP-09)*.

Ronald Langacker. 2008. *Cognitive grammar: A basic introduction*. OUP USA.

Todd Lubart. 2005. How can computers be partners in the creative process: Classification and commentary on the special issue. *International Journal of Human-Computer Studies*, 63(4):365 – 369. Computer support for creativity.

Ikujiro Nonaka. 1994. A dynamic theory of organizational knowledge creation. *Organization science*, 5(1):14–37.

Vasile Rus, Cristian Moldovan, Nobal Niraula, and Arthur C Graesser. 2012. Automated discovery of speech act categories in educational games. *International Educational Data Mining Society*.

John Rogers Searle. 1969. *Speech acts: An essay in the philosophy of language*. Cambridge university press.

Heinz Von Foerster. 2007. *Understanding understanding: Essays on cybernetics and cognition*. Springer Science & Business Media.

Alex W White. 2011. *The Elements of Graphic Design*. Allworth Press.

Geraint A Wiggins. 2006. A preliminary framework for description, analysis and comparison of creative systems. *Knowledge-Based Systems*, 19(7):449–458.

Georgios N Yannakakis, Antonios Liapis, and Constantine Alexopoulos. 2014. Mixed-initiative co-creativity. In *Proceedings of the 9th Conference on the Foundations of Digital Games*.

Automatic Dialect Adaptation in Finnish and its Effect on Perceived Creativity

Mika Hämäläinen[1]
mika.hamalainen@helsinki.fi

Niko Partanen[2]
niko.partanen@helsinki.fi

Khalid Alnajjar[3]
khalid.alnajjar@helsinki.fi

Jack Rueter[1]
jack.rueter@helsinki.fi

Thierry Poibeau[4]
thierry.poibeau@ens.fr

[1]Digital Humanities, [2]Finnish, Finno-Ugrian and Scandinavian Studies, [3]Computer Science, University of Helsinki, FI
[4]Lab. LATTICE, ENS/PSL & CNRS & Univ. Sorbonne nouvelle, FR

Abstract

We present a novel approach for adapting text written in standard Finnish to different dialects. We experiment with character level NMT models both by using a multidialectal and transfer learning approaches. The models are tested with over 20 different dialects. The results seem to favor transfer learning, although not strongly over the multi-dialectal approach. We study the influence dialectal adaptation has on perceived creativity of computer generated poetry. Our results suggest that the more the dialect deviates from the standard Finnish, the lower scores people tend to give on an existing evaluation metric. However, on a word association test, people associate *creativity* and *originality* more with dialect and *fluency* more with standard Finnish.

Introduction

We present a novel method for adapting text written in standard Finnish to different Finnish dialects. The models developed in this paper have been released in an open-source Python library[1] to boost the limited Finnish NLP resources, and to encourage both replication of the current study and further research in this topic. In addition to the new methodological contribution, we use our models to test the effect they have on perceived creativity of poems authored by a computationally creative system.

Finnish language exhibits numerous differences between colloquial spoken regional varieties and the written standard. This situation is a result of a long historical development. Literary Finnish variety known as Modern Finnish developed into its current form in late 19th century, after which the changes have been mainly in the details (Häkkinen 1994, 16). Many of the changes have been lexical due to technical innovations and modernization of the society: orthographic spelling conventions have largely remained the same. Spoken Finnish, on the other hand, traditionally represents an areally divided dialect continuum, with several sharp boundaries, and many regions of gradual differentiation from one municipality to another municipality.

Especially in the later parts of 21th century the spoken varieties have been leveling away from very specific local dialects, and although regional varieties still exist, most of the local varieties have certainly became endangered. Similar processes of dialect convergence have been reported from different regions in Europe, although with substantial variation (Auer 2018). In the case of Finnish this has not, however, resulted in merging of the written and spoken standards, but the spoken Finnish has remained, to our day, very distinct from the written standard. In a late 1950s, a program was set up to document extant spoken dialects, with the goal of recording 30 hours of speech from each municipality. This work resulted in very large collections of dialectal recordings (Lyytikäinen 1984, 448-449). Many of these have been published, and some portion has also been manually normalized. Dataset used is described in more detail in Section Data and Preprocessing.

Finnish orthography is largely phonemic within the language variety used in that representation, although, as discussed above, the relationship to actual spoken Finnish is complicated. Phonemicity of the orthography is still a very important factor here, as the differences between different varieties are mainly displaying historically developed differences, and not orthographic particularities that would be essentially random from contemporary point of view. Thereby the differences between Finnish dialects, spoken Finnish and Standard Finnish are highly systematic and based on historical sound correspondences and sound changes, instead of more random adaptation of historical spelling conventions that would be typical for many languages.

Due to the phonemicity of the Finnish writing system, dialectal differences are also reflected in informal writing. People speaking a dialect oftentimes also write it as they would speak it when communicating with friends and family members. This is different from English in that, for example, although Australians and Americans pronounce the word *today* differently, they would still write the word in the same way. In Finnish, such a dialectal difference would result in a different written form as well.

We hyphotesize that dialect increases the perceived value of computationally created artefacts. Dialectal text is something that people are not expecting from a machine as much as they would expect standard Finnish. The effect dialect has on results can be revealing of the shortcomings of evaluation methods used in the field.

---

[1]https://github.com/mikahama/murre

Related Work

Text adaptation has received some research attention in the past. The task consists of adapting or transferring a text to a new form that follows a certain style or domain. As the particular task of dialect adaptation has not received a wide research interest, we dedicate this section in describing different text adaptation systems in a mode broad sense.

Adaptation of written language to a more spoken language style has previously been tackled as a lexical adaptation problem (Kaji and Kurohashi 2005). They use style and topic classification to gather data representing written and spoken language styles, thereafter, they learn the probabilities of lexemes occurring in both categories. This way they can learn the differences between the spoken and the written on a lexical level and use this information for style adaptation. The difference to our approach is that we approach the problem on a character level rather than lexical level. This makes it possible for our approach to deal with out-of-vocabulary words and to learn inflectional differences as well without additional modeling.

Poem translation has been tackled from the point of view of adaptation as well (Ghazvininejad, Choi, and Knight 2018). The authors train a neural model to translate French poetry into English while making the output adapt to specified rhythm and rhyme patterns. They use an FSA (finite-state acceptor) to enforce a desired rhythm and rhyme.

Back-translation is also a viable starting point for style adaptation (Prabhumoye et al. 2018). They propose a method consisting of two neural machine translation systems and style generators. They first translate the English input into French and then back again to English in the hopes of reducing the characteristics of the initial style. A style specific bi-LSTM model is then used to adapt the back translated sentence to a given style based on gender, political orientation and sentiment.

A recent line of work within the paradigm of computational creativity presents a creative contextual style adaptation in video game dialogs (Hämäläinen and Alnajjar 2019). They adapt video game dialog to better suit the state of the video game character. Their approach works in two steps: first, they use a machine translation model to paraphrase the syntax of the sentences in the dialog to increase the variety of the output. After this, they refill the new syntax with the words from the dialog and adapt some of the content words with a word embedding model to fit better the domain dictated by the player's condition.

A recent style adaptation (Li et al. 2019) learns to separate stylistic information from content information, so that it can maximize the preservation of the content while adapting the text to a new style. They propose an encoder-decoder architecture for solving this task and evaluate it on two tasks; sentiment transfer and formality transfer.

Earlier work on Finnish dialect normalization to standard Finnish has shown that the relationship between spoken Finnish varieties and literary standard language can be modeled as a character level machine translation task (Partanen, Hämäläinen, and Alnajjar 2019).

Data and Preprocessing

We use a corpus called Samples of Spoken Finnish (Institute for the Languages of Finland 2014) for dialect adaptation. This corpus consists of over 51,000 hand annotated sentences of dialectal Finnish. These sentences have been normalized on a word level to standard Finnish. This provides us with an ideal parallel data set consisting of dialectal text and their standard Finnish counterparts.

The corpus was designed so that all main dialects and the transition varieties would be represented. The last dialect booklet in the series of 50 items was published in 2000, and the creation process was summarised there by Rekunen (2000). For each location there is one hour of transcribed text from two different speakers. Almost all speakers are born in the 19th century. Transcriptions are done in semi-narrow transcription that captures well the dialect specific particularities, without being phonetically unnecessarily narrow.

The digitally available version of the corpus has a manual normalization for 684,977 tokens. The entire normalized corpus was used in our experiments.

Dialect	Short	Sentences
Etelä-Häme	EH	1860
Etelä-Karjala	EK	813
Etelä-Pohjanmaa	EP	2684
Etelä-Satakunta	ES	848
Etelä-Savo	ESa	1744
Eteläinen Keski-Suomi	EKS	2168
Inkerinsuomalaismurteet	IS	4035
Kaakkois-Häme	KH	8026
Kainuu	K	3995
Keski-Karjala	KK	1640
Keski-Pohjanmaa	KP	900
Länsi-Satakunta	LS	1288
Länsi-Uusimaa	LU	1171
Länsipohja	LP	1026
Läntinen Keski-Suomi	LKS	857
Peräpohjola	P	1913
Pohjoinen Keski-Suomi	PKS	733
Pohjoinen Varsinais-Suomi	PVS	3885
Pohjois-Häme	PH	859
Pohjois-Karjala	PK	4292
Pohjois-Pohjanmaa	PP	1801
Pohjois-Satakunta	PS	2371
Pohjois-Savo	PSa	2344

Table 1: Dialects and the number of sentences in each dialect in the corpus

Despite the attempts of the authors of the corpus to include all dialects, the dialects are not equally represented in the corpus. One reason for this is certainly the different sizes of the dialect areas, and the variation introduced by different speech rates of individual speakers. The difference in the number of sentences per dialect can be seen in Table 1. We do not consider this uneven distribution to be a problem, as it is mainly a feature of this dataset, but we have paid attention to these differences in data splitting. In order to get proportionally even numbers of each dialect in the different data sets, we split the sentences of each dialect into training (70%), validation (15%) and testing (15%) the split is done after shuffling the data. The same split is used throughout this paper.

The dialectal data contains non-standard annotations that are meant to capture phonetic and prosodic features that are usually not represented in the writing. These include the use of the acute accent to represent stress, superscripted characters, IPA characters and others. We go through all characters in the dialectal sentences that do not occur in the normalizations, i.e all characters that are not part of the Finnish alphabets and ordinary punctuation characters. We remove all annotations that mark prosodic features as these are not usually expressed in writing. This is done entirely manually as sometimes the annotations are additional characters that can be entirely removed and sometimes the annotations are added to vowels and consonants, in which case they form new Unicode characters and need to be replaced with their non-annotated counterparts.

Automatic Dialect Adaptation

In order to adapt text written in standard Finnish to dialects, we train several different models on the data set. As a character level sequence-to-sequence neural machine translation (NMT) approach has been proven successful in the past for the opposite problem of normalization of dialectal or historical language variant to the standard language (see (Bollmann 2019; Hämäläinen et al. 2019; Veliz, De Clercq, and Hoste 2019; Hämäläinen and Hengchen 2019)), we approach the problem form a similar character based methodology. The advantage of character level models to word level models is their adaptability to out of vocabulary words; a requirement which needs to be satisfied for our experiments to be successful. In practice, this means splitting the words into characters separated by white-spaces and marking word boundaries with a special character, which is underscore (_) in our approach.

In NMT, language flags have been used in the past to train multi-lingual models (Johnson et al. 2017). The idea is that the model can benefit from the information in multiple languages when predicting the translation for a particular language a expressed by a language specific flag given to the system. We train one model with all the dialect data, appending a dialect flag to the source side. The model will then learn to use the flag when adapting the standard Finnish text the the desired dialect.

Additionally, we train one model without any flags or dialectal cues. This model is trained to predict from standard Finnish to dialectal text (without any specification in terms of the dialect). This model serves two purposes, firstly if it performs poorly on individual dialects, it means that there is a considerable distance between each dialect so that a single model that adapts text to a generic dialect cannot sufficiently capture all of the dialects. Secondly, this model is used as a starting point for dialect specific transfer learning.

We use the generic model without flags for training dialect specific models. We do this by freezing the first layer of the encoder, as the encoder only sees standard Finnish, it does not require any further training. Then we train the dialect specific models from the generic model by continuing the training with only the training and validation data specific to a given dialect. We train each dialect specific model in the described transfer learning fashion for an additional 20,000 steps.

Our models are recurrent neural networks. The architecture consists of two encoding layers and two decoding layers and the general global attention model (Luong, Pham, and Manning 2015). We train the models by using the Open-NMT Python package (Klein et al. 2017) with otherwise the default settings. The model with flags and the generic model are trained for 100,000 steps. We train the models by providing chunks of three words at a time as opposed to training one word or whole sentence at a time, as a chunk of three words has been suggested to be more effective in a character-level text normalization task (Partanen, Hämäläinen, and Alnajjar 2019).

Table 2 shows an example of the sequences used for training. The model receiving the dialect flag has the name of the dialect appended to the beginning of the source data, where as the generic model has no additional information apart from the character sequences. The dialect specific transfer learning models are also trained without an additional flag, but rather the exposure solely to the dialect specific data is considered sufficient for the model to better learn the desired dialect.

Results and Evaluation

In this section, we present the results of the dialect adaptation models on different dialects. We use a commonly used metric called word error rate (WER) and compare the dialect adaptations of the test sets of each dialect to the gold standard. WER is calculated for each sentence by using the following formula:

$$WER = \frac{S + D + I}{S + D + C} \qquad (1)$$

WER is derived from Levenshtein edit distance (Levenshtein 1966) as a better measurement for calculating word-level errors. It takes into account the number of deletions D, substitutions S, insertions I and the number of correct words C.

The results are shown in Tables 3 and 4. On the vertical axis are the models. *Flags* represents the results of the model that was trained with initial tokens indicating the desired dialect the text should be adapted in. *No flags* is the model trained without any dialectal information, and the rest of the models are dialect specific transfer learning models trained on the *no flags* model.

The results are to be interpreted as the lower the better, i.e. the lower the WER, the closer the output is to the gold dialect data in a given dialect. These results indicate that the *no flag* model does not get the best results for any of the dialects, which is to be expected, as if it reached to good results, that would indicate that the dialects do not differ from each other. Interestingly, we can observe that the transfer

	Source		Target
Flags	Inkerinsuomalaismurteet m i n ä _ k u n _ n ä i n		m i e _ k o _ n ä i n
No flags	m i n ä _ k u n _ n ä i n		m i e _ k o _ n ä i n

Table 2: Example of the training data. The sentence reads "when I saw" in English

model	EH	EK	EP	ES	ESa	EKS	IS	KH	K	KK	KP	LS
Flags	24.37	19.8	25.13	**28.09**	27.22	25.19	21.09	28.73	**25.56**	**24.59**	22.51	30.49
No flags	38.87	36.21	41.98	42.16	37.71	37.35	39.38	39.03	37.05	42.43	39.03	42.3
EH	**24.21**	43.6	37.64	35.77	46.83	42.98	51.51	41.05	42.38	53.26	38.95	37.53
EK	48.65	**19.28**	52.63	47.57	35.69	39.94	31.86	42.97	47.14	33.13	49.76	45.51
EP	38.8	50.37	**24.9**	42.3	49.2	46.3	54.47	46.39	44.71	55.68	39.21	44.24
ES	34.36	44.81	41.49	29.03	49.35	47.8	50.05	45.56	47.74	51.16	38.02	37.12
ESa	46.06	32.28	49.5	50.38	**26.81**	32.43	42.01	44.26	38.4	40.32	45.88	47.9
EKS	44.3	37.3	47.06	51.05	34.15	**25.07**	45.56	42.97	36.5	42.84	42.65	47.86
IS	52.09	28.4	55.13	49.53	41.52	44.57	**19.69**	41.13	50.24	29.14	52.26	46.65
KH	43.98	38.34	47.75	47.66	45.46	43.23	41.16	**28.43**	47.88	44.36	47.9	45.76
K	42.59	45.05	45.11	50.11	39.79	35.97	50.56	48.17	**25.56**	49.34	40.89	49.63
KK	54.1	30	55.59	51.52	40.52	43.12	29.21	43.65	49.74	24.87	53.52	50.21
KP	35.58	43.94	38.58	40.2	44.54	41.53	51.03	45.84	39.26	52.04	22.51	44.32
LS	36.05	39.56	42.77	35.73	46.21	45.34	47.7	43.4	46.73	48.19	40.76	**29.71**
LU	38.45	45.07	44.24	39.17	51.68	51.03	47.35	41.04	51.14	49.54	46.74	38.97
LP	40.58	44.55	42.07	41.94	46.1	44.94	49.32	46.35	44.42	50.71	35	44.57
LKS	33.25	40.03	37.48	39.88	39.42	35.24	49.09	42.59	43.99	49.82	32.79	42.64
P	39.05	44.38	40.83	42.72	45.09	42.25	50.06	46.11	41.1	51.14	35.12	44.34
PKS	45.73	43.03	48.96	51.9	36.41	33.39	48.55	47.2	33.37	46.73	43.46	52.63
PVS	50.34	41.51	52.91	44.13	50.96	53.29	44.48	46.03	55.99	46.38	53.35	43.09
PH	31.26	44.72	38.38	37.56	44.61	39.4	52.07	42.19	38.51	52.73	35.43	40.82
PK	44.14	44.33	47.18	50.83	36.98	37.08	46.76	46.09	33.51	46.5	42.58	51.05
PP	34.73	44.38	37.87	41.85	43.24	39.46	52	45.12	36.91	52.84	27.12	43.25
PS	28.42	46.29	35.51	36.62	46.96	42.46	53.15	41.84	42.31	53.84	36.63	38.6
PSa	43.12	40.86	47.81	49.71	34.74	33.12	46.47	44.95	32.01	45.44	45.28	51.15

Table 3: WER for the different models for dialects from Etelä-Häme to Länsi-Satakunta

learning method gives the best scores for almost all the dialect, except for Etelä-Satakunta (ES), Keski-Karjala (KK), Keski-Pohjanmaa (KP), Pohjois-Karjala (PK) and Pohjois-Satakunta (PS), for which the model with flags gives the best results. Both methods are equally good for Pohjois-Häme (PH). All in all, the difference between the two methods is rather small in the WER. An example of the dialectal adaptation can be seen in Table 5.

Based on these results it is difficult to suggest one method over the other as both of them are capable of reaching to the best results on different dialects. On the practical side, the model with dialectal flags trains faster and requires less computational resources, as the model is trained once only and it works for all the dialects immediately, where as transfer learning has to be done for each dialect individually after training a generic model.

Evaluation of the models with and without dialectal flags shows that especially in word forms that are highly divergent in the dialect, it is almost impossible for the model to predict the correct result that is in the test set. This doesn't mean that the model's output would necessarily be entirely incorrect, as the result may still be perfectly valid dialectal representation, it just is in a different variety.

There are also numerous examples of features that are in variation also within one dialect. In these cases the model may produce a form different from that in the specific row of a test set. These kind of problems are particularly prominent in examples where the dialectal transcription contains prosodic phenomena at the word boundary level. Since the model starts the prediction from standard Finnish input, it cannot have any knowledge about specific prosodic features of the individual examples in test data. Some phonologi-

cal features such as assimilation of nasals seem to be over-generalized by the model, and also in this case it would be impossible for the model to predict the instances where such phenomena does not take place due to particularly careful pronunciation.

Another interesting feature of the model is that it seems to be able to generalize its predictions into unseen words, as long as they exhibit morphology common for the training data. There are, however, instances of clearly contemporary word types, such as recent international loans, that have general shape and phonotactics that are entirely absent from the training data. The problems caused by this are somewhat mitigated by fact that in many cases the standard Finnish word can be left intact, and it will pass within the dialectal text relatively well.

This has a consequence that the scores reported here are possibly slightly worse than the model's true abilities. The resulting dialectal text can still be very accurate and closely approximate the actual dialect, although the prediction would slightly differ from the test instances. At the same time if the model slips into predicted text some literary Finnish forms, the result is still perfectly understandable, and also in real use the dialects would rarely be used in entire isolation from the standard language.

It must also be taken into account that only either a native dialect speaker or an advanced specialist in Finnish dialectology can reliably detect minute disfluencies in dialectal predictions, especially when the error is introduced by a form of other dialect. Similarly it would be very uncommon to have such knowledge about all the Finnish dialects the model operates on. After this careful examination of the models, we proceed to the generation of dialectal poems and

model	LU	LP	LKS	P	PKS	PVS	PH	PK	PP	PS	PSa
Flags	27.87	20.02	21.89	27.53	28.73	32.4	**20.03**	**27.15**	21.51	**21.56**	27.6
No flags	43.49	37.1	35.06	38.35	40.54	49.19	34.9	36.44	35.12	38.54	37.86
EH	39.9	35.63	33.65	39.92	48.42	51.05	27.61	41.9	32.54	27.46	43.91
EK	50.59	45.08	46.23	46.75	46.03	47.19	45.62	43.82	45.84	51.85	43.21
EP	47.04	37.78	39.13	41.56	52.06	56.16	33.28	44.64	34.32	35.23	46.35
ES	43.01	36.6	40.35	42.12	52.27	47.34	34.46	46.08	37.09	35.13	48.23
ESa	53.26	40.5	38.89	43.85	37.36	54.04	39.56	35.68	40.02	46.65	35.55
EKS	52.05	40.5	35.72	41.94	36.11	55.63	38.27	37.34	38.33	42.99	35.35
IS	48.72	47.29	49.67	48.39	49.59	45.74	49.89	46.45	48.51	54.29	46.18
KH	44.26	44.17	43.45	46.91	49.09	49.42	42.14	45.54	44.09	43.86	44.09
K	52.71	39.03	34.47	39.75	35.07	58.24	35.52	33.57	35.43	41.77	33.67
KK	51.83	48.19	50.94	49.37	49.41	48.7	50.84	45.66	50.27	55.14	45.86
KP	48.5	27.67	34.21	35.92	43.07	56.07	30.26	40.42	25.17	35.28	42.05
LS	42.57	36.9	39.88	42.58	51.71	47.31	34.74	46.31	38.71	36.28	47.7
LU	**25.9**	43.04	44.97	45.66	54.87	43.76	40.63	49.41	43.76	40.15	50.93
LP	49.41	**19.57**	38.2	32.23	47.75	55.87	35.04	43.57	33.96	37.92	45.85
LKS	45.39	33.2	**21.41**	34.97	40.88	55.13	26.9	36.47	28.22	31.57	36.37
P	47.29	28	35.54	**26.81**	46.23	56.06	33.45	40.98	32.7	37.82	43.27
PKS	55.67	41.86	39.87	42.62	**28.65**	57.68	39.28	35.8	38.08	46.01	33.67
PVS	46.42	49.26	54.99	52.31	57.36	**31.67**	52.13	52.69	51.34	53.44	53.39
PH	44.15	33.2	31.47	36.83	44.44	55.22	**20.03**	38.14	30.76	28.94	40.5
PK	53.77	41.01	38.61	42.59	38.34	57.18	37.99	27.28	37.87	46.02	34.98
PP	48.43	30.77	32.43	34.85	43.11	57.03	28.9	38.09	**21.04**	34.2	39.94
PS	42.17	35.18	32.03	38.9	47.14	54.2	26.49	41.34	31.54	22	42.98
PSa	52.19	42.13	36.28	42.45	35.29	56.52	38.29	32.8	37.67	43.96	**27.24**

Table 4: WER for the different models for dialects from Länsi-Uusimaa to Pohjois-Savo

their further evaluation by native Finnish speakers.

Effect on Perceived Creativity

In this section, we apply the dialect adaptation trained in the earlier sections to text written in standard Finnish. We are interested in seeing what the effect of the automatically adapted dialect is on computer generated text. We use an existing Finnish poem generator (Hämäläinen 2018) that produces standard Finnish (SF) text as it relies heavily on hand defined syntactic structures that are filled with lemmatized words that are inflected with a normative Finnish morphological generator by using a tool called Syntax Maker (Hämäläinen and Rueter 2018). We use this generator to generate 10 different poems.

The poems generated by the system are then adapted to dialects with the models we elaborated in this paper. As the number of different dialects is extensive and conducting human questionnaire with such a myriad of dialects is not feasible, we limit our study to three dialects. We pick Etelä-Karjala (EK) and Inkerinsuomalaismurteet (IS) dialects because they are the best performing ones in terms of WER and Pohjoinen Varsinais-Suomi (PVS) dialect as it is the worst performing in terms of WER. For this study, we use the dialect specific models tuned with transfer learning.

A qualitative look at the predictions revealed that the dialectal models have a tendency of over generating when a word chunk has less than three words. The models tend to predict one or two additional words in such cases, however, if the chunk contains three words, the models do not over nor under generate words. Fortunately this is easy to overcome by ensuring that only as many dialectal words are considered from the prediction as there were in the chunk written in standard Finnish. For instance *olen vanha* (I am old) gets predicted in IS as *olev vanha a*. The first two words are correctly adapted to the dialect, while the third word *a* is an invention by the model. However, the models do not systematically predict too many words as in *pieni ?* (small?)

to *pien ?* adaptation. For this reason, we only consider as many words as in the original chunks when doing the dialectal adaptation.

Replicating the Poem Generator Evaluation

In our first experiment, we replicate the poem generator evaluation that was used to evaluate the Finnish poem generator used in this experiment. We are interested in seeing whether dialectal adaptation has an effect on the evaluation results of the creative system. They evaluated their system based on the evaluation questions initially elaborated in a study on an earlier Finnish poem generator (Toivanen et al. 2012). The first evaluation question is a binary one *Is the text a poem?*. The rest of the evaluation questions are asked on a 5-point Likert scale:

1. How typical is the text as a poem?
2. How understandable is it?
3. How good is the language?
4. Does the text evoke mental images?
5. Does the text evoke emotions?
6. How much do you like the text?

The subjects are not told that they are to read poetry nor that they are reading fully computer generated and dialectally adapted text. We conduct dialectal adaptation to the 10 generated poems to the three different dialects, this means that there are altogether four variants of each poem, one in standard Finnish, and three in dialects. We produce the questionnaires automatically in such a fashion that each questionnaire has the 10 different poems shuffled in random order each time. The variants of each poem are picked randomly so that each questionnaire has randomly picked variant for each of the poems. Every questionnaire contains poems from all of the different variant types, but none of them contains the same poem more than once. Each questionnaire is unique in the order and combination of the variants. We

SF	EK	PVS	IS	Translation
himo on palo,	himo om palos,	himo om palo,	himo om palloo,	desire is a fire,
se syttyy herkästi	se syttyy herkäst	se sytty herkästi	se syttyy herkäst	it gets easily ignited
taas intona se kokoaa	taas intonna se kokovaa	taas inton se kokko	toas inton se kokohoa	again, as an ardor it shall rise
milloin into on eloisa?	millo into on elosa?	millon innoo on elosa?	millon into on eloisa?	when is ardor vivacious?
näemmekö me,	näämmekö met,	näämekö me,	neämmäks meä,	will we see
ennen kuin into jää pois?	enne ku into jää pois?	ennen ku into jää pois?	ennen ku into jää pois?	before ardor disappears?
mikäli innot pysyisivät,	mikäli innot pysysiit,	mikäl innop pysysivät,	mikält innot pysysiit,	if ardors stayed,
sinä huomaisit innon	sie huomasit inno	siä huamasit inno	sie huomaisit inno	you would notice the ardor
minä alan maksamaan innon	mie alan maksamaa inno	mää ala maksaman inno	mie ala maksamaa inno	I will start paying for the ardor
olenko liiallinen?	olenko siialli?	olenko liialline?	olenko liialine?	Am I extravagant?

Table 5: An example poem generated in standard Finnish and its dialectal adaptations to three different dialects

introduce all this randomness to reduce constant bias that might otherwise be present if the poem variants were always presented in the same order.

We print out the questionnaires and recruit people native in Finnish in the university campus. We recruit 20 people to evaluate the questionnaires each of which consisting of 10 poems. This means that each variant of a poem is evaluated by five different people.

Table 6 shows the results from this experiment, however some evaluators did not complete the task for all poems in their pile[2]. Interestingly, the results drop on all the parameters when the poems are adapted into the different dialects in question. The best performing dialect in the experiment was the Etelä-Karjala dialect, and the worst performing one was the Pohjoinen Varsinais-Suomi dialect all though it got the exact same average scores with Inkerinsuomalaismurteet on the last three questions. Now these results are not to be interpreted as that dialectal poems would always get worse results, as we only used a handful of dialects form the possibilities. However, the results indicate an interesting finding that something as superficial as a dialect can affect the results. It is to be noted that the dialectal adaptation only alters the words to be more dialectal, it does not substitute the words with new ones, nor does it alter their order.

In order to better understand why the dialects were ranked in this order, we compare the dialectal poems to the standard Finnish poems automatically by calculating WER. These WERs should not be understood as "error rates" since we are not comparing the dialects to a gold standard, but rather to the standard Finnish poems. The idea is that the higher the WER, the more they differ from the standard. Table 7 shows the results of this experiment. The results seem to be in line with the human evaluation results; the further away the dialect is from the standard Finnish, the lower it scores in the human evaluation. This is a potential indication of familiarity bias; people tend to prefer the more familiar language variety.

Word Association Test

In the second experiment, we are interested in seeing how people associate words when they are presented with a standard Finnish version and a dialectally adapted variant of the

same poem. The two poems are presented on the same page, labeled as A and B. The order is randomized again, which means that both the order of poems in the questionnarie and whether the dialectal one is A or B is randomized. This is done again to reduce bias in the results that might be caused by always maintaining the same order. The concepts we study are the following:

- emotive
- original
- creative
- poem-like
- artificial
- fluent

The subjects are asked to associate each concept with A or B, one of which is the dialectal and the other the standard Finnish version of the same poem. We use the same dialects as before, but which dialect gets used is not controlled in this experiment. We divide each questionnaire of 10 poems into piles of two to reduce the work load on each annotator as each poem is presented in two different variant forms. This way, we recruit altogether 10 different people for this task, again native speakers from the university campus. Each poem with a dialectal variant gets annotated by five different people.

Table 8 shows the results of this experiment. Some of the people did not answer to all questions for some poems. This is reflected in the *no answer* column. The results indicate that the standard Finnish variant poems were considered considerably more fluent than the dialectal poems, and slightly more emotive and artificial. The dialectal poems were considered considerably more original and creative, and slightly more poem-like.

It is interesting that while dialectal poems can get clearly better results on some parameters on this experiment, they still scored lower on all the parameters in the first experiment. This potentially highlights a more general problem on evaluation in the field of computational creativity, as results are heavily dependent on the metric that happened to be chosen. The problems arising from this "ad hoc" evaluation practice are also discussed by (Lamb, Brown, and Clarke 2018).

---

[2]The data is based on 47 observations for SF, 46 for EK, 43 for PVS and 49 for IS out of the maximum of 50.

	Poem	Typical			Understandable			Language			Mental images			Emotions			Liking		
	%	M	Mo	Me	M	Mo	Me	M	Mo	Me	M	Mo	Me	M	Mo	Me	M	Mo	Me
SF	87.2%	2.85	4	3	3.62	4	4	3.51	4	4	3.57	4	4	2.94	2	3	3.02	4	3
EK	82.6%	2.5	2	2	3	4	3	2.87	3	3	3.26	4	3	2.67	2	2	2.70	2	3
IS	77.6%	2.69	2	3	2.90	3, 4	3	2.78	2	3	3.27	4	3	2.86	2	3	2.61	3	3
PVS	77.0%	2.51	2	2	2.80	2	3	2.58	2	3	3.27	4	3	2.86	2	3	2.61	3	3

Table 6: Results form the first human evaluation. Mean, mode and median are reported for the questions on Likert-scale

	EK	IS	PVS
WER	34.38	43.41	54.69

Table 7: The distance of the dialectal poems form the original poem written in standard Finnish

	SF	Dialect	No answer
emotive	**48%**	46%	6%
original	40%	**60%**	0%
creative	32%	**64%**	4%
poem-like	46%	**50%**	4%
artificial	**50%**	46%	4%
fluent	**74%**	24%	2%

Table 8: Results of the second experiment with human annotators

Conclusions

We have presented our work on automatic dialect adaptation by using a character-level NMT approach. Based on our automatic evaluation, both the transfer learning method and a multi-dialectal model with flags can achieve the best results in different dialects. The transfer learning method, however, receives the highest scores on most of the dialects. Nevertheless, the difference in WERs of the two methods is generally small, therefore it is not possible to clearly recommend one over another to be used for different character-level data sets. If the decision is based on the computational power used, then the multi-dialectal model with flags should be used as it only needs to be trained once and it can handle all the dialects.

The dialect adaptation models elaborated in this paper have been made publicly available as an open-source Python library[3]. This not only makes the replication of the results easier but also makes it possible to apply these unique Finnish NLP tools on other related research or tasks outside of the academia as well.

Our study shows that automatic dialect adaptation has a clear impact to how different attributes of the text are perceived. In the first experiment that was based on existing evaluation questions, a negative impact was found as the scores dropped on all the metrics in comparison to the original standard Finnish poem. However, when inspecting the distance the dialects have from the standard Finnish, we noticed that the further away the dialect is form the standard, the lower it scores.

We believe that the low scores might be an indication of

___
[3]https://github.com/mikahama/murre

familiarity bias, which means that people have a tendency of preferring things they are more familiar with. Especially since the evaluation was conducted in a region in Finland with a high number of migrants from different parts of the country. This leads to a situation where the most familiar language variety for everyone regardless of their dialectal background is the standard Finnish variety. Also, as the dialectal data used in our model originates from the Finnish speakers born in the 19th century, it remains possible that the poems were transformed into a variety not entirely familiar to the individuals who participated into our survey. In the upcoming research it is necessary to investigate the perceptions of wider demographics, taking into account larger areal representation.

Based on our results, it is too early to generalize that familiarity bias is a problem in evaluation of computationally creative systems. However, it is an important aspect to take into consideration in the future research. We are interested in testing this particular bias out in the future in a more controlled fashion. Nevertheless, the fact that a variable, such as dialect that is never controlled in the computational creativity evaluations, has a clear effect on the evaluation results, raises a real question about the validity of such evaluation methods. As abstract questions on 5-point Likert scale are a commonly used evaluation methodology, the question of narrowing down the unexpected variables, such as dialect, that affect the evaluation results positively or negatively is vital for the progress in the field in terms of comparability of results from different systems.

Even though the initial hypothesis we had on dialects increasing the perceived value of computationally created artefacts was proven wrong by the first experiment, the second experiment showed that dialects can indeed have a positive effect on the results as well, in terms of perceived creativity and originality. This finding is also troublesome form the point of view of computational creativity evaluation in a larger context. Our dialect adaptation system is by no means designed to exhibit any creative behavior of its own, yet people are more prone to associating the concept *creativity* with dialectally adapted poetry.

The results of the first and second experiment give a very different picture of the impact dialect adaptation has on perceived creativity. This calls for a more thorough research on the effect different evaluation practices have on the results of a creative system. Is the difference in results fully attributable to subjectivity in the task, what was asked on how it was asked. Does making people pick between two (dialectal and standard Finnish in our case) introduce a bias not present when people rate the poems individually? It is important these questions be systematically addressed in the future research.

Acknowledgments

Thierry Poibeau is partly supported by a PRAIRIE 3IA Institute fellowship ("Investissements d'avenir" program, reference ANR-19-P3IA-0001).

References

Auer, P. 2018. Dialect change in europe–leveling and convergence. *The Handbook of Dialectology* 159–76.

Bollmann, M. 2019. A large-scale comparison of historical text normalization systems. In *Proceedings of the 2019 Conference of the North American Chapter of the Association for Computational Linguistics: Human Language Technologies, Volume 1 (Long and Short Papers)*, 3885–3898. Minneapolis, Minnesota: Association for Computational Linguistics.

Ghazvininejad, M.; Choi, Y.; and Knight, K. 2018. Neural poetry translation. In *Proceedings of the 2018 Conference of the North American Chapter of the Association for Computational Linguistics: Human Language Technologies, Volume 2 (Short Papers)*, 67–71.

Häkkinen, K. 1994. *Agricolasta nykykieleen: suomen kirjakielen historia*. Söderström.

Hämäläinen, M., and Alnajjar, K. 2019. Creative contextual dialog adaptation in an open world rpg. In *Proceedings of the 14th International Conference on the Foundations of Digital Games*, 1–7.

Hämäläinen, M., and Hengchen, S. 2019. From the paft to the fiiture: a fully automatic nmt and word embeddings method for ocr post-correction. In *Recent Advances in Natural Language Processing*, 432–437. INCOMA.

Hämäläinen, M., and Rueter, J. 2018. Development of an open source natural language generation tool for finnish. In *Proceedings of the Fourth International Workshop on Computational Linguistics of Uralic Languages*, 51–58.

Hämäläinen, M.; Säily, T.; Rueter, J.; Tiedemann, J.; and Mäkelä, E. 2019. Revisiting NMT for normalization of early English letters. In *Proceedings of the 3rd Joint SIGHUM Workshop on Computational Linguistics for Cultural Heritage, Social Sciences, Humanities and Literature*, 71–75. Minneapolis, USA: Association for Computational Linguistics.

Hämäläinen, M. 2018. Harnessing nlg to create finnish poetry automatically. In *International Conference on Computational Creativity*, 9–15. Association for Computational Creativity (ACC).

Institute for the Languages of Finland. 2014. Suomen kielen näytteitä - Samples of Spoken Finnish [online-corpus], version 1.0. http://urn.fi/urn:nbn:fi:lb-201407141.

Johnson, M.; Schuster, M.; Le, Q. V.; Krikun, M.; Wu, Y.; Chen, Z.; Thorat, N.; Viégas, F.; Wattenberg, M.; Corrado, G.; Hughes, M.; and Dean, J. 2017. Google's multilingual neural machine translation system: Enabling zero-shot translation. *Transactions of the Association for Computational Linguistics* 5:339–351.

Kaji, N., and Kurohashi, S. 2005. Lexical choice via topic adaptation for paraphrasing written language to spoken language. In *International Conference on Natural Language Processing*, 981–992. Springer.

Klein, G.; Kim, Y.; Deng, Y.; Senellart, J.; and Rush, A. M. 2017. OpenNMT: Open-Source Toolkit for Neural Machine Translation. In *Proc. ACL*.

Lamb, C.; Brown, D. G.; and Clarke, C. L. 2018. Evaluating computational creativity: An interdisciplinary tutorial. *ACM Computing Surveys (CSUR)* 51(2):1–34.

Levenshtein, V. I. 1966. Binary codes capable of correcting deletions, insertions, and reversals. *Soviets Physics Doklady* 10(8):707–710.

Li, D.; Zhang, Y.; Gan, Z.; Cheng, Y.; Brockett, C.; Sun, M.-T.; and Dolan, B. 2019. Domain adaptive text style transfer. *arXiv preprint arXiv:1908.09395*.

Luong, M.-T.; Pham, H.; and Manning, C. D. 2015. Effective approaches to attention-based neural machine translation. *arXiv preprint arXiv:1508.04025*.

Lyytikäinen, E. 1984. Suomen kielen nauhoitearkiston neljännesvuosisata. *Virittäjä* 88(4):448–448.

Partanen, N.; Hämäläinen, M.; and Alnajjar, K. 2019. Dialect text normalization to normative standard finnish. In *Proceedings of the 5th Workshop on Noisy User-generated Text (W-NUT 2019)*, 141–146.

Prabhumoye, S.; Tsvetkov, Y.; Salakhutdinov, R.; and Black, A. W. 2018. Style transfer through back-translation. In *Proceedings of the 56th Annual Meeting of the Association for Computational Linguistics (Volume 1: Long Papers)*, 866–876. Melbourne, Australia: Association for Computational Linguistics.

Rekunen, J. 2000. *Suomen kielen näytteitä 50*. Kotimaisten kielten tutkimuskeskus.

Toivanen, J.; Toivonen, H.; Valitutti, A.; and Gross, O. 2012. Corpus-Based Generation of Content and Form in Poetry. In *Proceedings of the Third International Conference on Computational Creativity*.

Veliz, C. M.; De Clercq, O.; and Hoste, V. 2019. Benefits of data augmentation for nmt-based text normalization of user-generated content. In *Proceedings of the 5th Workshop on Noisy User-generated Text (W-NUT 2019)*, 275–285.

Development of an Open Source Natural Language Generation Tool for Finnish

Mika Hämäläinen
University of Helsinki
Department of Modern Languages
mika.hamalainen@helsinki.fi

Jack Rueter
University of Helsinki
Department of Modern Languages
jack.rueter@helsinki.fi

Abstract

We present an open source Python library to automatically produce syntactically correct Finnish sentences when only lemmas and their relations are provided. The tool resolves automatically morphosyntax in the sentence such as agreement and government rules and uses Omorfi to produce the correct morphological forms. In this paper, we discuss how case government can be learned automatically from a corpus and incorporated as a part of the natural language generation tool. We also present how agreement rules are modelled in the system and discuss the use cases of the tool such as its initial use as part of a computational creativity system, called Poem Machine.

Tiivistelmä

Tässä artikkelissa esittelemme avoimen lähdekoodin Python-kirjaston kieliopillisten lauseiden automaattista tuottamista varten suomen kielelle. Kieliopilliset rakenteet pystytään tuottamaan pelkkien lemmojen ja niiden välisten suhteiden avulla. Työkalu ratkoo vaadittavan morfosyntaktiset vaatimukset kuten kongruenssin ja rektion automaattisesti ja tuottaa morfologisesti oikean muodon Omorfin avulla. Esittelemme tavan, jolla verbien rektiot voidaan poimia automaattisesti korpuksesta ja yhdistää osaksi NLG-järjestelmää. Esittelemme, miten kongruenssi on mallinnettu osana järjestelmää ja kuvaamme työkalun alkuperäisen käyttötarkoituksen osana laskennallisesti luovaa Runokone-järjestelmää.

1   Introduction

Natural language generation is a task that requires knowledge about the syntax and morphology of the language to be generated. Such knowledge can partially be coded

The source code is released in GitHub https://github.com/mikahama/syntaxmaker

Proceedings of the 4th International Workshop for Computational Linguistics for Uralic Languages (IWCLUL 2018), pages 51–58,
Helsinki, Finland, January 8–9, 2018. ©2018 Association for Computational Linguistics

by hand into a computational system, but part of the knowledge is better obtained automatically such as case government for verbs.

Having a computer create poetry automatically is a challenging task. Even more so in the context of a morphologically rich language such as Finnish which makes generating grammatical sentences, even when they are not creative, a challenge. Therefore having a syntactically solid system as a part of the poem generation process is extremely important.

In this paper, we present an open-source tool for producing syntactically correct Finnish sentences. This tool is used as a part of an NLG pipeline in producing Finnish poetry automatically. The poem generation part of the pipeline is out of the scope of this paper.

2 Related work

Previously in the context of poetry generation in Finnish (Toivanen et al., 2012), the problem of syntax has been solved by taking a ready-made poem, analyzing it morphologically and replacing some of the words in it, inflecting them with the morphology of the original words. This, however, does not make it possible to generate entirely new sentences, and it fails to take agreement or government rules into account, instead it expects agreement and government to be followed automatically if words with sufficient similarity are used in substitutes.

Another take on generating Finnish poetry in a human-computer co-creativity setting (Kantosalo et al., 2015) was to use sentences extracted from the Project Gutenberg's children's literature in Finnish. These sentences were treated as "poetry fragments" and they were used to generate poems by combining them together in a randomized fashion. This method indeed gives syntactically better results than the one described in (Toivanen et al., 2012), as it puts human-written sentences together, but it doesn't allow any variation in the poem apart from the order of the sentences in the poem.

Reiter (1994) identifies four different steps in an NLG pipeline. Those are content determination, sentence planning, surface generation, and morphology and formatting. In the content determination step, an input is given to the NLG system, e.g. in the form of a query to obtain desired information from the system. Based on this query, a semantic representation is produced addressing the results to the query. In other words, this step decides what information is to be conveyed to the user in the final output sentence, but also how it will be communicated in the rhetorical planning of the sentence.

The sentence planner will then get the semantic representation as input and produce an abstract linguistic form which contains the words to be used in the output and their syntactic relations. This step bears no knowledge of how the syntax will actually be realized, i.e., agreement or government rules, instead it applies the chosen words and how they are related to one another.

The last two steps of the pipeline deal with the actual realization of the syntax in the sentence. It is the task of the surface generator to handle the linguistic expression of the abstract linguistic structure. It means resolving agreement, forming questions in a syntactically correct manner, negation and so on. The actual word forms required are produced in the morphology step.

3 The Finnish NLG tool

The tool, Syntax Maker, described in this paper focuses on the surface generation step of the NLG pipeline described by Reiter (1994). It is used as a part of a complete NLG pipeline for producing Finnish poetry and is currently in place in the Poem Machine[1] system. This tool was made as a part of the poem generation system in order to solve the problem of creating novel, grammatical sentences not tackled by the previous Finnish poem generators. Taking an NLG point of view hasn't been studied before in the case of Finnish poetry, which is a shame since Finnish, unlike English, has a rich morphosyntax. This rich morphosyntax must be given proper attention if the computational creativity system is to be given more freedom to produce sentences of its own, using its own choice of words in a sentence that might cause other words around them to undergo morphological change as dictated by agreement and government.

Syntax Maker only knows the morphology needed in the level of tags. For example, it knows what case to use for a noun and what person to use for a verb. Actual morphological forms are generated using Omorfi (Pirinen et al., 2017).

3.1 Syntactic representation

Syntax Maker is designed to take the abstract linguistic structure of a sentence as its input. This structure consists of part-of-speech specific phrases each of which have their head word in lemmatized form. The phrases are nested under each other so that the highest possible root of the tree is a verb phrase.

When the phrases are nested together, they need to be added in proper slots to fulfill the requirements of agreement and government. For example, a noun phrase that is to act as a direct object of a verb phrase has to be nested in the verb phrase slot *dir_object*. In dealing with verb phrases, Syntax Maker automatically deduces the possible slots based on the verbs used as heads. In other words, Syntax Maker, determines the valency of a verb automatically and assigns values such as transitive, ditransitive or intransitive. On an abstract level, the phrases and their structures are defined manually.[2]

Using phrase structures gives us an easier way to implement the needed functionalities. Since the structure of phrases is similar for different parts-of-speech, we can reuse the same code across different parts-of-speech. The division into part-of-speech specific phrases gives us more freedom in expressing their peculiarities such as agreement and government rules and what kind of phrases can be nested under them. These structures come with a predefined word order, but it's not enforced by Syntax Maker. In other words, the word order in a phrase can be shuffled at will without losing the government or agreement information. Even with an altered word order, Syntax Maker can resolve the proper morphology correctly. The phrase structures are defined in JSON outside of the source code of Syntax Maker written in Python.

3.2 Handling government

Case government rules for adpositions have been hand coded. This can be attributed to the fact that there is only a very limited number of adpositions in Finnish, and it takes little time for a native speaker to write down the case required of a noun

---

[1] http://runokone.cs.helsinki.fi/

[2] These structures are available on https://github.com/mikahama/syntaxmaker/blob/master/grammar.json

53

phrase when it serves as complement to a given adpositional phrase. The analogous treatment of verbs, however, would be overly time consuming and laborious, and hence this has been automated.

As Finnish is an accusative language, the object is marked with a specific case. The case used depends on the verb in question and thus has to be specified for each verb separately. We obtain the case government information together with verb transitivity automatically from The Finnish Internet Parsebank (Kanerva et al., 2014) syntactic bi-grams.

Each line of the automatically parsed Parsebank bi-gram data consists of two word forms connected by a syntactic relation in the order in which they appeared in the sentence. These word forms are accompanied by their lemma, part-of-speech, morphology and syntactic annotation.

To extract the cases in which nouns have been linked to verbs, we look for lines in which the first word form has *V* as its part-of-speech tag and the second word form has *N* part-of-speech and *NUM_Sg* in its morphology. The reason why we limit the search to singular nouns only is that, in Finnish, a verb that takes its object in genitive in singular, takes it in nominative in plural, e.g. *syön kakun* and *syön kakut* but not **syön kakkujen*. Therefore taking plural objects into account as well would introduce more undesired complexity. Furthermore, we ignore all nouns where the lemma and word from are the same. This is done because the noun in question would then either be in the nominative, which is not an object case, or it will have been given an improper analysis in which case no lemmatization has been performed. Examples of this kind of wrong analyses in the corpus are *kattella/kattella/N/NUM_Sg* and *kasteleen/kasteleen/N/NUM_Sg*. For each bi-gram filling these criteria, we store the lemma of the verb and the case the related noun was in. This gives us a dictionary[3] of verbs and frequencies for noun cases associated with each verb.

The resulting dictionary is then used to determine the transitivity of a verb and the most frequent case for its object(s). This dictionary consists also of a plethora of non-verbs such as *Ljubuški* and *Dodonpa* as a result of erroneous parsing in the Parsebank data. This, however, causes no problems in the system because the dictionary also contains a extensive number of real, lemmatized verbs. Given that Syntax Maker operates on the level of surface generation, it is not actively involved in choosing the words in the NLG task. This means that, unless Syntax Maker is specifically instructed to use a non-verb it happens to know as a verb, it won't. This noise in the verb noun case dictionary, however, has no real effect on the grammaticality of the generated sentences.

The transitivity and most frequent case of the object is determined for a given verb by the verb noun case dictionary. The system is coded to accept the genitive, partitive, elative and illative as possible direct object cases and the essive, translative, ablative, allative and illative cases as indirect object cases. When the system defines whether a verb can take a direct object, it requires the relative frequency of one of the direct object cases to be above 23% of all the possible cases the verb has been seen with. For ditransitivity, the threshold is 18% for an indirect object case. Ditransitivity will not be considered if the verb is determined not to have a direct object. These threshold values have been adjusted by hand after looking at the performance of the system with a handful of verbs used in testing.

The genitive serves another use in Finnish syntax in addition to marking the direct

---

[3] The verb-noun case dictionrary is released on `https://github.com/mikahama/syntaxmaker/blob/master/verb_valences_new.json`

object. If the most frequent direct object case is genitive, we preform an additional check to see that it really is being used as an object function. The verb has to also has enough partitive case, over 23%, so that we can safely say that genitive indeed can be used as an object. This is because in Finnish, verbs that take their direct object in the genitive, also accept partitive in certain contexts such as in the expression of differences in aspect or negation.

3.3 Modelling agreement

Agreement, unlike government, is something that does not need to be extracted from a corpus. It is a rather straightforward thing and can be modelled with hand-written rules. In Finnish the predicate verb agrees in person and number with the subject, and adjective attributes agree in case and number with the head noun.

Since all the phrase types in our system are modelled in a similar way, it is easy to introduce agreement rules in the phrase structures. In a phrase structure, we define a key that is either *parent* referring to the parent phrase of the current phrase or a key to the list of *component*. Component lists all the possible syntactic positions for nested phrases such as *subject* or *dir_object*. Even though there aren't many agreement relations in Finnish, by modelling them in the external grammar file, we hope to make it easier to add more languages to the system in the future.

When Syntax Maker produces a sentence, it starts to process the syntactic tree phrase by phrase. For each phrase, it looks at the defined agreement relationship and copies the morphological information from the phrase defined to be agreed with. The agreement relation in the grammar file states the morphological tags which should be copied, for example in the case of an adjective phrase, the tags are *CASE* and *NUM*.

3.4 Modifying the verb phrase

Apart from just providing basic grammaticality by resolving agreement and government, Syntax Maker also provides means to modify verb phrases to produce more complex, yet grammatical sentences.

Syntax Maker can be used to negate sentences. When a sentence is negated, a new phrase with the head *ei* is added to the components of the verb phrase as *aux*. The new phrase has an agreement relation *parent->subject: PERS, NUM* and the verb phrase containing the predicate verb is tagged as *NEG* so that it will be conjugated as such when the full sentence is produced as text. The case of the direct object is also changed to partitive if the most frequent direct object case of the verb is genitive, in compliance with Finnish grammar.

Mood and tense are also handled by Syntax Maker. In the case of the prefect, the auxiliary verb *olla* is set as the new head of the verb phrase and the old head is moved to a new subordinate phrase with the part-of-speech value *PastParticiple* and agreement *parent->subject: NUM*. This makes sense from the point of view of Syntax Maker since *olla* is the verb that is conjugated normally while the participle form only agrees with the number of the subject. Other auxiliary verbs can be added in a similar fashion, where the auxiliary verb substitutes the original head and the verb is moved to a nested phrase with the morphology required by the auxiliary verb.

Passive voice is handled by creating a dummy phrase as a subject with the morphological tags *PERS = 4* and *NUM = PE*. This will automatically make the verb agree with the dummy phrase's morphology and produce the correct form as output. Also, if the verb takes its direct object in genitive, the government rule is changed so that the direct object will be in the nominative.

A sentence can also be turned into an interrogative one. This adds an additional morphological tag *CLIT = KO* to the head of the verb phrase and moves it to the beginning of the whole sentence. Syntax Maker does not produce punctuation, so a question mark has to be appended to the end of the sentence at a different level in the NLG pipeline.

4 Evaluation

In this part, we evaluate how accurately Syntax Maker can produce verb phrases. We limit this evaluation to the automatically extracted information used by Syntax Maker because it is more prone to errors than the hand written rules. This means that we are evaluating two things in the generated output: the predicted valency i.e. how many objects the verb can take and the predicted case for the object.

In order to do the evaluation, we take a hundred Finnish verbs at random from the Finnish Wiktionary[4]. These verbs are then given as input to Syntax Maker to produce verb phrases out of them. The valency and object cases are then checked by hand to conduct the evaluation phase.

	too low	too high	correct
valency prediction	28%	5%	67%

Table 1: Accuracy in predicting valency

Syntax maker predicts the number of objects correctly 67% of the time and 28% of the time too low. This is acceptable in the task of poem generation where we are interested in generating syntactically correct poems. Having too few objects in the generated output only creates an ellipsis that doesn't result in incorrect syntax. However, in other NLG tasks outside of the scope of poem generation, the objects might be important and thus having a higher accuracy is something to work towards.

	case correct	case incorrect	no object
object case prediction	50%	4%	46%

Table 2: Accuracy in predicting object case

In the test set, Syntax Maker produced a wrong case only 4% of the time. 46% of the verbs were either truly intransitive or didn't take an object according to Syntax Maker. In other words, by just taking into account the transitive verbs recognized by Syntax Maker, the accuracy reached to 93%. This means that Syntax Maker is very good at coming up with the correct case but not as good at determining the valency accurately.

5 Future work

At the current state, Syntax Maker doesn't handle all parts of the Finnish grammar. For instance, it doesn't have the functionality to express aspectual difference by alter-

---

[4] From a Wiktionary dump on `https://dumps.wikimedia.org/fiwiktionary/`

ing between genitive and partitive objects. In addition, it has only a limited knowledge of the transitivity of verbs. Novel automated ways should be studied to solve this shortcoming.

In the future, Syntax Maker should be tested as a part of the NLG pipeline in uses other than poetry generation as well. This might reveal new requirements for the system that do not appear in the task of poetry generation. This might also reveal missing functionalities both in the generation of syntax and the API provided by the library that are needed in other NLG tasks.

Including small Uralic languages in this tool is also in our interest for the future. This is because having an NLG system would be especially useful in the case of minority languages, for example in generation of news automatically in these languages.

6   Conclusions

In this paper we have presented an open source Python library called Syntax Maker. The library was made to be used as a low-level syntax producer in a new NLG pipeline for producing Finnish poetry and is currently in place in a computational creativity system known as Poem Machine[5]. By embracing the notion of separation of concerns in the software architecture of the system, Syntax Maker can be used in a multitude of contexts outside of computational creativity applications as an all-purpose tool for producing grammatical Finnish. To achieve this goal, a method for extracting the information needed to resolve verbal agreement automatically was presented and evaluated.

Acknowledgments

This work has been supported by the Academy of Finland under grant 276897 (CLiC)

References

Jenna Kanerva, Juhani Luotolahti, Veronika Laippala, and Filip Ginter. 2014. Syntactic n-gram collection from a large-scale corpus of internet finnish. In *Proceedings of the Sixth International Conference Baltic HLT*.

Anna Kantosalo, Jukka Toivanen, and Hannu Toivonen. 2015. Interaction evaluation for human-computer co-creativity: A case study. In *Proceedings of the Sixth International Conference on Computational Creativity*. pages 276–283.

Tommi A Pirinen, Inari Listenmaa, Ryan Johnson, Francis M. Tyers, and Juha Kuokkala. 2017. Open morphology of finnish. LINDAT/CLARIN digital library at the Institute of Formal and Applied Linguistics, Charles University. http://hdl.handle.net/11372/LRT-1992.

Ehud Reiter. 1994. Has a consensus nl generation architecture appeared, and is it psycholinguistically plausible? In *Proceedings of the Seventh International Workshop on Natural Language Generation*. INLG '94.

---

[5] Poem Machine can be used on http://runokone.cs.helsinki.fi/

Jukka Toivanen, Hannu Toivonen, Alessandro Valitutti, and Oskar Gross. 2012. Corpus-based generation of content and form in poetry. In *Proceedings of the Third International Conference on Computational Creativity*.